FOR THE CONVERSION OF THE CHURCHES

Groupe des Dombes

FOR THE CONVERSION OF THE CHURCHES

*An independent group
of Catholics and Protestants
in France issues a challenge
to the divided churches:
to recognize that their identity
is grounded in a continual
conversion – without which
their unity can never be realized*

WCC Publications, Geneva

Translated from the French by James Greig

Cover design: Rob Lucas

ISBN: 2-8254-1123-X

© 1993 English translation WCC Publications, World Council of Churches, 150 route de Ferney, 1211 Geneva 2, Switzerland

Original title *Pour la conversion des Eglises*
© 1991 Editions du Centurion, Paris

Printed in Switzerland

Table of Contents

Preface *Konrad Raiser*	ix
Outline of argument	1
I. Clues for a Terminology	5
II. A Glance at History	7
III. The Witness of Scripture	8
IV. Final Suggestions	11
Introduction	13
Part I: Identity and Conversion: Clues for a Terminology	17
I. Some Paradoxes on Identity in General	17
II. Christian, Ecclesial and Confessional Identities	19
a) Christian identity	19
b) Ecclesial identity	21
c) Confessional identity	22
III. Christian, Ecclesial and Confessional Conversion	25
a) Christian conversion	26
b) Ecclesial conversion	26
c) Confessional conversion	27
d) Balance-sheet	29
Part II: Examples from History	30
Introduction	30
I. The Ancient Church and the Medieval Church	30
a) Three examples of conversion *(metanoia)* in the ancient church (fourth-fifth centuries)	30
b) The "conversions" of St Augustine (354-430)	33
c) Identity without conversion: theocratic hardening and the breach between East and West (ninth-fourteenth centuries)	36
d) Balance-sheet	40

    II. The Church at the Beginning of the Modern Age   40
        a) The Protestant Reformation   40
        b) The Catholic reform   45
        c) From confessions of faith to confessionalism
           (seventeenth-eighteenth centuries)   50
        d) Balance-sheet   53
    III. The Ecumenical Movement: Conversion Underway   55
        a) Conversion at the source of the ecumenical movement   55
        b) Conversion underway   58
        c) Balance-sheet   63

Part III: The Witness of Scripture   66
    a) Repentance and conversion   66
    b) Identity and identities   67
    c) Identity, renunciation and conversion   69
    d) Balance-sheet   75

Part IV: Final Recommendations   76
    I. The Four Marks of the Church: Invitation to Conversion   76
    II. Our Respective Temptations   80
    III. For a Competitive Approach in Conversion   82
        a) A call to the churches of the Protestant Reformation   82
        b) A call to the Roman Catholic Church   83
        c) A call to all our churches   85

Appendix: Some Simple Suggestions for Catechesis Where There Is Conversion   87

Notes   91

Identity and Change in the Dynamics of Communion

Let the same mind be in you as was in Christ Jesus,
who, though he was in the form of God,
did not regard equality with God
as something to be exploited,
but emptied himself,
taking the form of a slave,
being born in human likeness.
And being found in human form,
he humbled himself
and became obedient to the point of death —
even death on a cross.
Therefore God also highly exalted him
and gave him the name
that is above every name,
so that at the name of Jesus
every knee should bend,
in heaven and on earth and under the earth,
and every tongue should confess
that Jesus Christ is Lord
to the glory of God the Father.
                            Philippians 2:5-11

Preface

Since its founding in 1937 by the Abbé Paul Couturier — who is perhaps best known in ecumenical circles as the guiding spirit behind the Week of Prayer for Christian Unity — the Groupe des Dombes has made unique and significant contributions to the effort to overcome the spiritual and theological alienation that continue to divide the churches. An anthology of the Group's reports, *Pour la communion des Eglises*, published in 1988 to mark its fiftieth anniversary, displays the richness of the insights that have emerged from its discussions, whose ecumenical influence has been widespread, even if the Group itself remains too little known, even to many ecumenists, outside France.

A reading of the texts assembled in that anniversary volume makes it clear that the hope for the "conversion of the churches" — the opening of themselves to unity — has been a pervasive stimulus for the work which the Groupe des Dombes has undertaken. Recognition that making visible the unity of the now-divided churches will demand just such a turning, a change of heart and mind, is reflected in the Decree on Ecumenism of the Second Vatican Council, which portrays it as the "soul of the whole ecumenical movement" (*Unitatis Redintegratio*, 7-8). It has been echoed often by theologians, ecumenists and church leaders, but perhaps most insistently by Christians in local situations. Deeply committed to working and worshiping across ancient lines of division, they are perplexed and frustrated that hard-won statements of convergence on doctrinal issues have not been followed by clearer evidence of the unity which all confess.

The present book, translated from the French, is the fruit of an intensive examination undertaken by the Groupe des Dombes of this key motif of conversion. Its starting point is the conviction that a genuine *convergence* between the churches can happen only if all churches, individually and together, turn themselves anew to their Lord Jesus Christ in *conversion*. As a famous statement of the first Life and Work conference (Stockholm, 1925) has it, the closer we come to the crucified Christ, the closer we come to each other.

Inevitably, of course, the call for such a conversion of the churches runs headlong into a formidable obstacle: the fear on the part of every church that in the process it would lose its own cherished identity. A key insight in the pages that follow is that identity as a Christian or as a church is ultimately rooted in precisely such a movement of conversion, a turning again to the common centre, so that this identity can remain living and authentic only through a continuing conversion. Thus the way to unity passes through the conversion of the churches, exactly at that point where they feel themselves strong and certain of their convictions.

The text develops this basic thesis in four chapters. With considerable nuance, the first outlines an understanding of identity and conversion and how they are inter-related on the personal, churchly and confessional levels. The second chapter seeks historical verification for this, taking up several key moments in church history up to the rise of the ecumenical movement in this century. The third chapter goes into the many-faceted biblical vocabulary bearing on the subject. Finally, the fourth chapter sets forth some lines for ecumenical praxis, in which the call for a common confession of "one, holy, catholic and apostolic church" serves as the norm.

Within these four chapters the reader will encounter a wealth of valuable insights, many of which deserve even fuller investigation than is possible within so brief a compass. But what is finally most significant about this book is the way it seeks to go beyond what might be called a mere "moral" judgment on the contemporary ecumenical situation — yet another protest at the "scandal" of division — and beyond a mere passionate call for the conversion of the churches to offer a theological interpretation of the inter-relationship of identity and conversion as constitutive poles in the course of Christian and churchly existence.

I believe this is crucial for the ongoing ecumenical discussion of ecclesiology. I trust that the availability of an English translation of this provocative and significant little volume will make it possible for many more people to join in what is a critically important discussion at this moment of ecumenical history.

KONRAD RAISER
General secretary
World Council of Churches

Outline of Argument

I

No one is in any doubt that the churches must be converted to their Lord. But in saying this, one is usually thinking of the conversion of each Christian individually or of the Christian community in its entirety.

This book is addressed to the Roman Catholic and Protestant churches in order to invite them to converge in converting together to the Lord. Thus once more the ecumenical impulse itself is at the source of the questions raised by the Groupe des Dombes: the Christian communities will come closer to each other with clarity of mind if they are faithful to their Lord and draw near to him.

If this is so, that very clarity will lead to an initial acknowledgment that the common faith of the churches is expressed in traditional credal "symbols" (the Apostles' Creed and the Nicene-Constantinopolitan Creed), but also in particular confessions (the Augsburg Confession and the Confession of La Rochelle, for instance, or Paul VI's confession of faith). The Roman Catholic and the Protestant churches adhere to the traditional symbols. Only the Christian community concerned with a particular confession of faith adheres to it. Hence we may ask what is the situation of the Christian, Catholic or Protestant, before the churches' common confession of faith and before the confession of faith which affirms the special character of his or her church and establishes thereby that a Roman Catholic is not a Protestant?

The pilgrimage of a Christian towards God is what defines him or her as a Christian. We might say that one's identity is the course which one follows. To describe oneself by saying with Sanctus, the martyr of Lyons, "I am a Christian", is to undergo a conversion to God, confessing with Augustine of Hippo, "You have made us for yourself and our heart is restless till it finds rest in you." Christian identity is conversion to God.

Is this constant turn-about of one's whole self — expressed in the gospel by the word *metanoia*, which we translate as "conversion" or "repentance" — enough to ensure that the church itself constantly converts to the Lord? Does the continual conversion of each member suffice to renew the whole body? There are of course those who will say that the church must always be reformed. This *ecclesia semper reformanda*, however, is perhaps not still today the cry of hope of the entire church, because some but not all Christians recognize themselves in the designation "Reformed". For this scandal to come to an end, ecclesial conversion is called for, both of the Roman Catholic and the Reformation churches (not to mention the other churches which were not represented in the work we have done).

The Lord calls on all of them to recognize their identity by confessing their error in the renewal of their evangelical and apostolic faith and not in rigidly standing unchanged in their own particular confessions.

Does this mean that the specific expressions of faith in Christ — which in fact have a separating effect — must disappear? Put more plainly, must one cease to be a Catholic in order to be a Christian, or cease to maintain that one is a Protestant in order to affirm one's loyalty to Christ? According to one's temperament — authoritarian, juridical or diplomatic — one could translate the same refusal by a "no", a "no, because...", or a "yes, but...", whether downright, supported by evidence or calculating. It would undoubtedly be better to reply that confessional identities too must be converted in order to be faithful to themselves.

Here undoubtedly we touch on the most sensitive point. We are so accustomed — in a far from routine way — to live on the basis of a specific confession that to interfere with it causes disorientation and poses a threat to identity. This is why the conversion of the Christian confessions can emerge only from each of them. It is in experiencing their Christian identity in these confessions, and at the same time in dialogue with the other — recognized as a brother or sister — that disunited Christians will see where they are the same and where they differ, sometimes converging and sometimes diverging. This very divergence may then seem legitimate and not injurious to communion in Christ. We may also consider it divisive, but prefer a shaky marriage to a divorce with wrongs on both sides.

It will be said that these are figures of speech and deceptive comparisons. True; but the document that follows has not taken this line of least resistance and runs the risk of being censured for it. It has been worked out — and with what care! — by people moulded into working together in this way, who have their own ways of expressing themselves, indeed, their own obsessions and oddities. And perhaps it has found it hard to "keep things simple". In any event, the variety of sensitivities and styles will not fail to become evident in the chapters of this book as one reads on. We are nevertheless convinced that an attentive and somewhat well-disposed reader will understand what we have been doing together, and the ecumenical concern in our comments.

And if some should confine themselves to skimming through this work we would ask them to retain this from it: the Groupe des Dombes believes that the divisive character of the confessions of faith that belong to the Roman Catholic and the Reformation churches is not final. It can and must disappear. Doubtless it survives, but it has had its day. The plurality, certainly, must not disappear, but it is the duty of Christians to do everything to ensure that it is compatible with unity and communion *(koinonia)*. The Group even offers some quite practical hints to this effect.

II

This new document of the Groupe des Dombes — the sixth since 1979 and the most extensive to date — is therefore entitled *For the Conversion of the Churches*. With this title the Group is trying to take up the challenge addressed to it during its fiftieth anniversary in 1987. Its original method — in the spirit of its founder, the Abbé Couturier — consists in calling for concrete acts of *metanoia* from the churches involved in ecumenical dialogue. This Greek word, which combines the ideas of repentance and conversion, was chosen to stress that the unity "as Christ wishes and by the means which he desires" must pass by way of the conversion of the churches, just where they feel themselves strongest and most assured in their conviction.

Some have considered this urgent call by the Groupe des Dombes — which is found in all its major documents — as a threat to the identity of the churches, and thus to be rejected out of the loyalty and obedience of each church to its Lord.

In the present document the Group replies to that by a counter-challenge. What appears to be a contradiction in terms is actually solidarity: there is no identity without conversion; *a fortiori* Christian identity could not be constituted and sustained, either personally or ecclesially, without constant and continued conversion. That is the price of Christian identity. Conversion is at the heart of this.

Essentially, *metanoia* is not aimed here at failings or marginal faults — of which the churches must also repent. It concerns their confessions of faith, precisely where the churches call themselves in the fullest sense of the term "Catholic" or "Orthodox" or "Protestant", but also where these designations concern apparently non-negotiable elements of their faith.

Thus the Groupe des Dombes has chosen another starting-point for the turn-about which it seeks to propose to the churches. While the theme of conversion occurs repeatedly in the Bible — to the point of defining the substance of Christian faith and life — the modern term "identity" does not appear there. Identity and conversion can only be centred in attitudes of faithfulness, truth and obedience; that is, always in relation to another, in particular to that Other who is himself "the way, the truth and the life" to lead us to the Father. Thus identity in the biblical sense consists in "turning" constantly towards that Other who himself turns constantly towards his God and Father in turning towards human beings who are his brothers and sisters (cf. Phil. 2:5-11).

Even in the practical details of the ecclesial life of Christian congregations, this fundamental and foundational Christian attitude can establish a dynamic of conversion which will not fail to work for the reconciliation and unity of the entire body of Christ.

III

The present document moves through four stages:

I. CLUES FOR A TERMINOLOGY (nos 10-55)

The document begins by examining the words on which this issue hinges: identity and conversion. It starts from the findings of the social sciences that there is no identity which is independent of an external or prior point of reference, or which can establish itself without that other still unfinished external element: the future, which is always open. Thus to cope with the fluctuations of constantly changing circumstances it is not enough to refer to a normative past, even if one adapts it by faithfulness to the spirit more than by adherence to the letter. We have to take account of a process of becoming, because of a future which has not yet materialized and without which identity is not achieved.

Identity is a "construction", a "pilgrimage". It dismisses an integrism or fundamentalism that harks back to the past, is concerned only about security and denies the other and the future. Equally it dismisses the opposite — a cutting loose from one's moorings and the relentless pursuit of a confused pluralism. The conversion in question here is "an essential constituent of an identity which seeks to remain alive and, quite plainly, faithful to itself" (no. 14).

The Groupe des Dombes, true to its method, distinguishes separate focuses of identity and conversion in order to give them fruitful and relevant expression. Thus we differentiate among identities and conversions described, in turn, as *Christian*, *ecclesial* and *confessional*:

Christian identity — and hence *Christian conversion* which gives it its foundation and form — consists in the mystery of "God's fatherly initiative in communicating himself to human beings by sending his Son Jesus Christ and bestowing his Holy Spirit" (no. 17); the corresponding conversion will be the appropriation by faith and the implementation of that mystery, which baptism inaugurates and celebrates: "It is a grace which opens onto a task" (no. 39).

Ecclesial identity — and consequently the corresponding *ecclesial conversion* — means that the church is the body of Christ where "by reason of the gift of the Spirit... the irreversible and unfailing presence of the gift God has given of himself to human beings in Jesus Christ" (no. 22) is made manifest — although the church is at the same time a community. That is why "ecclesial identity must always place itself in the service of Christian identity" (no. 25). Thus ecclesial conversion is constitutive of ecclesial identity.

Finally *confessional identity* — and consequently *confessional conversion* — relates to the particular form and mode each church has of confessing its faith. Historically, if each church seeks to be the church of Jesus Christ in its uniqueness and wholeness, that claim, once the churches confront each other, ends in mutual rejection; and confessional status then changes into "confessionalism", to the point that Christian identity amounts to ecclesial identity, which in turn amounts to confessional identity — Roman Catholic, Eastern Orthodox, Protestant/Evangelical (cf. no. 32). Confessionalism has brought about or revealed division, overturning the order of priority of the three identities and conversions (cf. no. 112). Reconversion from this consists in restoring these three motifs — all legitimate and all to be safeguarded — to their normal order of priority. But the divisive factor in them must after all become — or again become — a complementary difference, without which the "fullness and universality" of the church (no. 30) are seriously compromised. Instead of seeking "to safeguard its own identity jealously" (no. 32) at this narrow level, it is appropriate that each confession rediscover faithfulness to the gospel.

Conversion on this level is the most arduous because it is the most down-to-earth: how are we to confess our limitations and inadequacies — that is, the "sin" — of our own confessional family, which is still incapable of receiving and integrating genuine elements of Christian tradition that are nevertheless attested in our partners (cf. no. 47)? Confessional conversion will be achieved only when reconciliation has led to full communion with the others and "full mutual ecclesial recognition" (no. 51), through a purification and deepening in each confession in line with the gospel. This is what is at stake in the ecumenical movement today.

II. A GLANCE AT HISTORY (nos 56-154)

These preliminary reflections are then tested by an extended historical verification. In this part, which is easier to follow, we proceed by skimming and taking soundings; the aim is to show by examples that in the early church, prior to the great divisions, it was possible to hold on to the truth without being rigid about formulas which were nevertheless recognized as true. This is an attitude which is now acknowledged to be well-founded (cf. nos. 60-63). Conversely, we see the different churches when separated each exclusively claiming Christian faithfulness and authenticity, erecting allegiance to its own institutions or doctrines into the "unique and decisive criterion for belonging to the church" (cf. no. 77). This was true of the excessive power accorded to the papacy and to the centralization of the Roman church in the middle ages, which prevented the East from knowing where it stood (cf. nos 73-81). It was also true of the outcome of the effort at reform in the sixteenth century, which failed precisely at the level of ecclesiology because of mutual intransigence: some equated the church with the Roman church as such, others related it to the invisibility of the body of Christ.

Not until the nineteenth and especially the twentieth century, as the ecumenical movement took hold, did the churches, finally "filled with the concern for reconciliation" (no. 125), reach a crucial turning-point, turning towards each other and all together towards their one Lord, the only Son of the Father, in the unity of the Holy Spirit.

Thus the gestures of repentance, acts of conversion, documents of convergence, whose number continues to grow, are all so many signs, symbols and challenges which should involve the churches wholeheartedly.

This long historical summary will in fact have shown not only that identity and conversion are compatible but conversely that when they are at variance with each other unity is broken, truth wounded and the gospel which is entrusted to the church betrayed.

This does not entail the sacrifice of legitimate difference but a quest for a path which no longer makes it appear as divisive divergence. But achieving the discernment necessary for this can only be an adventure undertaken together in the ecumenical movement: unity lies at the end of the road only if it is at the very heart of that adventure.

III. THE WITNESS OF SCRIPTURE (nos 155-178)

Before moving on to the specific calls for the conversion of the churches we must recall the witness of scripture. But why so late in the document? Protestants at the very least will be disconcerted to see it appear so far on. Has the die not been cast already?

Here we have to take into account two aspects which are in a sense part of the actual movement of conversion within the Groupe des Dombes. In its previous documents, the Group has reflected on the place of scripture in the church and the establishment of a canon recognized by the churches themselves, structured as they are (cf. *Le ministère de communion dans l'Eglise universelle*, nos 15-23). This encounter between scripture and church means that scripture does not fall onto a *tabula rasa*, apart from the historical circumstances which shaped it and those who received it. Moreover, the present document refers to the "process of reception" which is an integral part of the constitution of a document accepted as authoritative (cf. no. 148).

But another aspect must be taken into account. Scripture has authority not through a kind of mechanical automatic operation but through situational analogies, normative models, examples that constrain us and meaningful figures and parables.

In short, in these instances the theme of conversion is so central and constant throughout scripture that it would have been necessary to set it out in all its fullness — an impossible task, which in any case goes beyond our purpose. Our concern was to show that the very movement of God towards human beings and of humanity's return to God became incarnate and was revealed in him who was God's representative to humanity, the face of God turned constantly towards human beings, the man of God, the Son of Man always turned towards God his Father, as he is portrayed in Philippians 2:5-11 (cf. nos 164-168).

It therefore seemed more fruitful to take soundings on meaningful wholes, to mark out a course, to suggest paths for research. What is crucial is a re-reading of scripture together in relation to its own internal coherence and in dialogue between what is said and what is heard, a statement and a reception, echoing the way scripture teaches the church.

Thus, taking into account a finer distinction between the two linked and previously mixed senses of *metanoia* as repentance and conversion (cf. no. 156), the former must be reserved for that movement of turning back on oneself, or rather to the foundation, which responds to a call — or recall — from God, while "conversion" refers rather to the active, positive implementation of a new way of thinking and living in openness to the future.

To take a central **example** from salvation-history, conversion is offered to the heathen when they decide for the gospel as something new, but the Jews for their part have to go by a path of repentance. Thus at the moment when believers of different origins are reconciled in a single church, renunciation and conversion will not have the same significance: it is one thing to renounce certain demands of the law, another to give up one's idols. The identity of each must be converted — spiritual repentance for the Jew, a veritable conversion for the heathen (cf. no. 162). In those two instances of course we have to do with dominant features, but they are significant.

It is no less true that here, too, Christian identity will not cease to be based on the otherness of its origins. Although the present document has not been able to deal with the problem of the special relations between the church and Israel, this concern has been put on record in a note drafted with that in mind.

While devoting a section (nos 164-168) to that divine identity of Christ which paradoxically consists in the otherness through which he reveals God by renouncing his equality with God — since he is already "Lord with the name above every name" when he appears as the Servant — the document offers the counter-proof of this by elaborating the meaning of the well-known parable of the two sons in Luke 15 (no. 172): how is the younger son's identity confirmed in the changes to which it is subjected? This son keeps the image of the Father imprinted on his inmost being and from this draws the capacity to come back, in order to dedicate it in a wholly new way, converted as if by rebirth — something of which his older brother still has no experience.

Scripture also shows us that in the very process of asserting one's identity, one runs the risk of betraying it. Thus it was with Peter, who was given a new name and a new identity, but betrayed it in tempting Jesus. So it can be with the church (nos 174-175).

Finally there is the repeated symbol of Jesus's physical gestures of turning, now in judgment, now in mercy (no. 167). These indicators in the text are not trivial.

This brief foray into the Bible may have been able to confirm that "conversion is the very opposite of loss of identity" (no. 178). Hence nothing can exempt the church from submitting to repentance as to something which "will lead it to its final identity".

IV. FINAL SUGGESTIONS (nos 179-221)

This long exposition ought to lead effectively into practical suggestions for conversion, not only out of faithfulness to a tradition and a method firmly established in the Groupe des Dombes but also because it is the very thing at stake in the present document, its moment of truth.

Before taking up specific points, a final step back will equip us better for the leap from conversion to unity. The touchstone considered is the church's confession of itself in the creed as "one, holy, catholic and apostolic". We draw attention to the fact that only the first two terms are biblical, the other two being derivative (no. 181). Consequently there is occasion to examine again how each of the churches has organized its "catholicity and apostolicity" in line with the fundamental requirement and gift of unity and holiness; some err by going too far, others by not going far enough. Here in regard to the four marks of the church we find again a reversed order of priorities — already rejected earlier — and denunciation of divergences of meaning and practice. All the churches — each in its own way — forget that their affirmations of identity depend on the original gift and the mission entrusted to them by him who does not cease to be their Saviour and exclusive mediator. An implicit twofold split turns the external marks and institutional authorities of the church into unseemly manifestations of power and illegitimate forms of autonomy. Sacralization and secularism are the two evils of a church which confuses privilege and service. True catholicity is of the gospel, true apostolicity is missionary.

On this foundation it is up to each church to examine its conscience, knowing that its "'inalienable share of truth' is always liable to be the point of its own perversion"; the place where its identity takes root is also the place of temptation (no. 195).

Moreover, the document lists the respective divergences which are apparently contrary, but emerge out of the same internal process of reversing priorities and relations of dependence, in particular between the three identities and conversions outlined above.

These proposals move from a common translation of the creed to the removal of the mutual anathemas of the past; from the resumption of the fine name "catholic" by the churches of the Reformation, whose origin goes back to the apostles, the fathers and the councils, to the recognition by the Roman Catholic Church of the authenticity of their ministries in terms of the gospel; from awareness of the gaps in a Protestant ecclesiology to the recognition of itself as an imperfect sacrament by the Catholic church which is historically marked by a "sin which places it in a fellowship of repentance with the other churches" (no. 211); from the affirmation of the normative character of scripture to that of the necessary visibility of the church which it founds and which obeys it.

In an appendix we have imagined — with a touch of humour — a Catholic and a Protestant hand in turn mischievously inserting into the catechism of the other church a page which expresses its own faith with full confidence and candour.

The document ends with a series of practical suggestions made to each of the parties concerned and a joint appeal to all the churches to enter the dynamic of confessional conversion as a contribution to the progressive realization of full communion among them: "in this way confessional conversion will serve ecclesial conversion and enable the church to give a credible witness to its conversion to Christ" (no. 221).

After the meeting of the Groupe des Dombes
held 3-7 September 1990

Alain Blancy	Maurice Jourjon
Protestant co-chairman	Roman Catholic co-chairman

Introduction

1. In February 1937 the Abbé Paul Couturier, supported by the Abbé Laurent Rémillieux, founded the Groupe des Dombes together with Rev. Richard Bäumlin. The aim was to set up a cell for prayer and doctrinal work among Roman Catholics and Protestants. Thus the Groupe des Dombes received its distinctive vocation: to look in prayer and dialogue for paths of convergence which would enable our churches to be reconciled with each other and arrive at unity in faith.

2. During its fifty years of existence, the Group has made an experiment in common life, listening to each other and sharing doctrinal and pastoral concerns, seeking to open itself to the best of its ability to the inspiration of the Holy Spirit. The requirement of conversion, which was already present in the Abbé Couturier's spiritual purpose, was not only a hope or a hypothesis but was becoming an experienced reality and a movement of the spirit and the heart which was leading us to new discoveries. At the same time we were becoming aware that the conversion of the churches which are at present divided is an urgent necessity of the Christian faith.

3. Three major stages in the life of our Group have revealed the progress of the attitude of conversion. In an initial stage the Group lived in a situation of face-to-face encounter, accepting in mutual goodwill one another's witness to the faith. We were thus led to walk side by side, which made it possible to work out a joint comment on some points of our doctrinal controversies.[1] Thus the very development of this conversion dynamic has enabled us to set out together whole chapters of ecumenical theology testifying to growing doctrinal reconcilia-

tion.² In this way we have experienced a real "ecumenical communion".

4. It is because we have experienced the fruitfulness of the act of conversion, like many other ecumenical groups, that we have been anxious to include it in our documents and let our readers share it. And so we have regularly created our documents on the basis of patterns of doctrinal conversion. As we wanted to embody — to incarnate — the results of our convergences in the life of the churches, we have often ended our documents with invitations for the conversion of our respective churches.

5. At the end of this half century our Group has felt the need and necessity to reflect on the theological foundations of the experience of conversion. At the same time several churches were raising with us this crucial question: Would the step of conversion which you are proposing not tend to the impoverishment, even loss, of our respective confessional identities? In experiencing this conversion can the churches be faithful to the faith they have inherited? We have been deeply aware of this important concern, and the question has been at the centre of our work on this new document.

6. But to speak of conversion at once causes resistance. Some kinds of resistance are due to problems of conscience, because of the necessary faithfulness to the confession of faith which each of us has received from our churches. Others are spontaneous, very human instances of psychological reluctance, caused by fear of losing our familiar religious landmarks. All of us are more inclined to look for the conversion of others than to work on our own.

7. What, then, is our Group's function? It certainly does not involve authority. The Groupe des Dombes, aware of its private nature, knows that its work has only the value that the churches are willing to grant it.

Our role is rather in the nature of witnessing, summoning and exhorting. In committing ourselves to the path of conversion and reconciliation we hope to encourage those who read our documents and their churches to contribute to this genuine process of "spiritual emulation", which, together with missionary urgency, lies behind the whole contemporary ecumenical movement.

8. We must begin by stating the conviction that was the object of our discovery and which underlies all the proposals that follow. *Far from excluding each other, identity and conversion call for each other: there is no Christian identity without conversion; conversion is constitutive of the church; our confessions do not merit the name of Christian unless they open up to the demand for conversion.*

* * *

9. This is how our argument will develop:

First of all we shall clarify some basic terms: Christian, ecclesial and confessional identities; Christian, ecclesial and confessional conversions. We shall thus suggest a certain linguistic convention necessary to make clear what we have in mind.

Second, some historical soundings will correspond to four aims:
— to show that the church throughout its existence has known movements of reform and conversion which really are part of its self-awareness;
— to record the benefits from these conversions as well as the failures, mistakes or instances of inflexibility they may have occasioned;
— to facilitate a common reading of our history, which is necessary to heal the wounds of our common and divided past;
— to discover in this way the road to conversion which can result in full visible communion.

We have always been conscious of the need to be guided by the witness of scripture. That is why the hymn addressed to the Philippians appears as the epigraph to our document. The very nature of our work, however, made us decide to appeal formally to scripture only *at a third stage*, in the shape of a theological re-reading and a process of verification. These will enable us to make the point that the requirement of a conversion that is necessary for identity finds its roots, as well as its models and norm, in God's self-revelation in the life of his people.

A fourth and last stage will bring out some key points of the conversion *(metanoia)* which awaits the churches today.

Part I
Identity and Conversion: Clues for a Terminology

I. SOME PARADOXES ON IDENTITY IN GENERAL

10. Anthropologically speaking, an identity is a living reality: it is a concrete expression of continuity and change. On the one hand, our identity always has to do with our origins. Our identity card or passport carries the name and surname we have received from our parents. Our birth certificate defines us as the son or daughter of such and such a person. Thus identity refers back to a history which precedes us; it makes us what we are in advance of ourselves. It also initiates a continuity through time: we live out our personal identity by taking on our original identity and all the determinants that accompany it, about which we can do nothing.

This continuity, moreover, does not have the static, fixed nature of something that is there once and for all. We have to live on this foundation imposed on us, and we progressively build an identity of our own which transforms our original identity even while respecting it. The harmony in our identity depends on how we manage to incorporate in dynamic unity those elements which have been imposed and those which depend on our freedom.

11. What is true of the individual person applies in a certain way to collective and social identities. In our age we have seen a certain disquiet in regard to collective identities. In this unsettled world, where the markers of personal existence and the contexts of social existence are constantly called in question, many no longer know where they are or who they really are. It is possible to speak of an identity crisis in a certain number of social or religious activities. Many react to this crisis by relating

once again to the original elements of identity. Genealogical researches, requests for regional and cultural identities, returning to traditional customs, etc. — which are necessary to allow individuals and groups to relate to their history and express what they are — can become regressive if they arise out of the desire for a nostalgic restoration of the past. Thus we are living in a time of vigorous reaffirmation of threatened identities with all that is positive and negative involved in that. This phenomenon may also assume the significance of a necessary transitional element within a process of healthy adaptation to the modern age.[3]

12. A collective identity is always a paradoxical phenomenon. In fact it embraces a tension between the effort of unification, integration, harmonization and social interaction (the quest for cohesion among the group members) on the one hand and the effort to differentiate and demonstrate uniqueness on the other hand — the group marks itself out by differentiating itself from the other groups or even by opposing them; in trying to be different it is itself. But this group must also become part of a much larger totality in order to be recognized by the other groups. Such mutual recognition is a necessary element in establishing an identity.

The quest for identity takes place in a journey which never reaches its destination, for this destination is confused with the ideal which the group's aspirations are constantly aiming to achieve. An identity which comes to a halt or becomes rigid is corrupted and ultimately lost. A living identity is never in fact perfected: it is always under construction. Only the future will disclose our identity conclusively.

13. The phenomenon of a quest for the security of our identity is also manifested in the religious sphere. Here the tendency is revealed by a renewal of "integrisms" or fundamentalisms — Muslim, Jewish and Christian. Christian fundamentalism is spread among the different confessions — Catholic, Protestant and Orthodox. These forms of fundamentalism have in common a rejection of the ecumenical movement, for that movement seems to represent a fundamental danger to a confessional identity which aims at being hardline and undiluted.

The typical feature of all forms of fundamentalism is their clinging to the values and customs of the past, without distinguishing the essential from the secondary. Everything is equally sacralized and absolutized; and sometimes the most exterior aspects, which are inherently also the most transient (dress, details of ritual, etc.), become the symbol of affirming an intransigent and even sectarian identity.

14. This is the standpoint from which we wish to propose a reflection that will define as clearly as possible what we understand by the different expressions of Christian, ecclesial and confessional identities. It is our conviction here that *conversion is an essential constituent of an identity which seeks to remain alive and, quite plainly, faithful to itself*. For this reason we want to deal with Christian, ecclesial and confessional conversions as being all part of the same process.

Our reflection may consequently take on the appearance of a kind of lexicon. But attention to the words will not make us forget either the down-to-earth realities we have in view — which differ from one confession to another — or the ecumenical problems which this kind of perspective raises.

II. CHRISTIAN, ECCLESIAL AND CONFESSIONAL IDENTITIES

a) Christian identity

15. At first sight it seems difficult to distinguish Christian identity from ecclesial identity. These two expressions really apply to the same concrete reality. But they do so from two different perspectives which deserve special reflection.

16. The term "Christian" expresses the relation which unites the believer to the person of Christ. Thus Christian identity is constituted by an existential confession of faith in relation to Christ, which is enshrined in the trinitarian confession and professed in church.[4]

17. A supplementary way to express Christian identity is to state the "Christian differentia", i.e. what makes Christianity essentially different from other religions. The dif-

ference consists in God's fatherly initiative in communicating himself to human beings by sending his Son Jesus Christ and bestowing his Holy Spirit. Thus the gospel mystery of Jesus, which we contemplate in his human life, his passion and the Easter event of his resurrection, is part and parcel of the difference.

18. This identity may be understood more comprehensively on the basis of the *symbolum*, creed or confession of faith expressed in the sacramental celebrations of the church and elaborated in a body of doctrine which concerns not only salvation-history but also the church. We then come up against the delicate question of the "hierarchy of truths".[5] The ecumenical problem arises immediately, for the confessions do not all have the same way of looking at what belongs to full Christian identity.

19. Existentially, Christian identity is not static but dynamic. It is a shifting of the centre, an exodus, a transition, a paschal movement. Christian identity is always a Christian becoming. It is an opening up to an eschatological beyond which ceaselessly draws it forward and prevents it from shutting itself up in itself. Thus it is a radical opening up to others beyond all the walls of separation. In its very essence it therefore contradicts the fixed or intransigent need for a secure identity. The existence in the church of the living Tradition, which is creative in its very faithfulness, has illustrated this constantly through the centuries.

20. Christian identity does not deny differences. It does not set itself up against others. It respects the identity of others and places its own specific difference in the service of a universal communion.

21. In fact Christian identity is not only dialogue or relationship, it is also service, *diakonia*. Its primary point of reference is the Servant Christ — he who washed the feet of his disciples. Christian identity is operative in acts of service. It is displayed in kenosis ("renunciation" and "self-emptying") — "Seek first the kingdom of God and his righteousness" (Matt. 6:33), and — we might add — Christian identity will be yours as well.

b) Ecclesial identity

22. While the doctrine about the church is not the ultimate truth of Christianity, nevertheless the church of Jesus Christ has something to do with Christian identity. The fact of the church and the belonging to it of each Christian are aspects of that identity.

This reflection makes it possible to distinguish (without separation) between Christian identity and ecclesial identity. For the church, seen simultaneously as a mystery and a community *(societas)*, awareness of its identity is an awareness that here and now in the midst of the world, in its local congregations, it is the church founded by and on Jesus Christ, who died and rose again. By reason of the gift of the Spirit it is like the irreversible and unfailing presence of the gift God has given of himself to human beings in Jesus Christ. Even if this belief is still the subject of ecumenical debate, it is present in every church.

23. Ecclesial identity is also an eschatological gift. While prior to us as a gift, it is one for which we have to be continually asking. Ecclesial identity thus necessarily sets up a tension between the now, the present, and the future, the goal. No confessional church can be identified as it stands with the church of Jesus Christ. In this sense ecclesial identity is the very goal of the ecumenical movement: "May the church be fully the church!"

24. Putting it differently, ecclesial identity is in labour for catholicity. Every church must become more "catholic" in the original sense of the term: full and universal.[6] The catholicity of all the churches is a wounded catholicity. Thus ecclesial identity opens up a large area for conversion.

25. Moreover if we take into account the idea of the *ecclesia semper reformanda* ("the church is always to be reformed"),[7] we must acknowledge that the church is the place of an encounter where God's faithfulness and human unfaithfulness cannot be disentangled. This situation creates a certain gap, even a conflict, between ecclesial identity as it is experienced and Christian identity as it is proclaimed. Without the church ever getting out of reach of the promises of salvation, it is

vulnerable to the givens of psychosociology. It can experience distortions, by-products of its real identity (partisan forms, a superiority complex, collective sin, etc.). It can always — as a body and in each of its members — become obscurantist and even contradict the Christian message of which it is the bearer. There we have an area open for conversion. Ecclesial identity must always place itself in the service of Christian identity.

c) Confessional identity

26. The distinction between ecclesial and confessional identity is not universally accepted. The different churches spontaneously claim that their confessional identity is ecclesial identity, "full stop". Thus the *Roman Catholic* Church has never understood nor defined itself theologically as a confession. It sees itself as that in which the one church of Christ "subsists";[8] it defines itself as the "communion" of that church. It can therefore accept being regarded as one Christian confession among others only from an historical and sociological point of view (in particular from the political standpoint since the sixteenth century).

27. Likewise the *Orthodox* church claims in its inmost conviction and ecclesial consciousness to be the custodian of and witness to the faith and Tradition of the one, holy, catholic and apostolic church. It considers itself as filling a central place in the world of today for matters relating to the progress of Christian unity. It rejects the idea of the equality of confessions, and what it equates with "confessional readjustment" cannot in its view constitute the unity of the church. In its view, God calls all Christians to the unity of the faith as this is experienced in the mystery and Tradition that is within the Orthodox church.[9]

28. On the side of the churches of the *Reformation*, the term "confession" has a much stronger weight than just a confessional "denomination". "Confession" designates not only a Christian community which presents itself with its own original characteristics among others, but also and especially the confession of faith which seeks to define its ecclesial and Christian identity and which expresses itself in a body of

"confessional" documents. "Confession" here is therefore the yardstick of a "confessing church" because it refers us to the one subject and object of faith: Jesus Christ. Thus it has normative value. That which is "confessional" in this theological sense then becomes the yardstick for ecclesial and Christian conversion.

29. Confessional identity lies in a specific historically, culturally and doctrinally located way of living out ecclesial identity and Christian identity. It is the typical "profile" of a group of churches, the common way in which these churches understand their spiritual specificity. Even if this profile undergoes changes in the course of history, a confessional constant remains which resists differences in time and place.

This identity is not only defined by theological characteristics and the marks of ecclesial structure; it also has to do with liturgical life, expressions of personal devotion and moral stances. Each confessional identity gives special prominence to certain specific aspects of the gospel message and of the "common life" of Christians.

30. To be genuine in Christian terms, a confessional identity must include fullness and universality. These two words must be understood in the sense of the calling, the mission and the inheritance received from the faith. For each confession is immersed in a Tradition that goes beyond its own confessional tradition.

31. But we cannot forget that confessional identities crystallized in history as a result of the occurrence of divisions. Each of the parties doubtless thought it could justify its position for reasons of faith and faithfulness to the original Christian message. Because of this it stressed certain positive elements. But the emergence of these new identities gave rise to certain manifestations of rejection of and aggressiveness towards the way other Christians were living out their Christian and ecclesial identities. These rejections contributed to a certain extent to giving the new identities their public image; and in polemical contexts they reappear to the point of sometimes seeming more crucial than aspects which are properly those of the gospel. The defence of confessional identities has caused wounds, as on

living tissue, which are not characteristic of the confession itself, still less of Christianity.

32. The words we use tell us about this reality by distinguishing between "confessional allegiance" *[confessionalité]* and "confessionalism". Confessional allegiance is the recognition of belonging to an historic church. Ecumenical dialogue requires that the partners should be truly rooted in their own confessions. And it is a good thing that Christians should be grateful for their specific spiritual inheritance and should wish to share it with the members of other confessions in order to enrich the exchanges among different types of Christians. Confessionalism is the hardening of confessional identity into an attitude of self-justification. Confessionalism, also called "denominationalism", withdraws into itself and rejects real confrontation with other confessions or denominations. Without going to this extreme, each, even in ecumenical dialogue, is tempted to safeguard its own identity jealously and to be little open to the share of truth present in its partner.

33. In the history of the ecumenical movement, confessional or denominational identity has sometimes been harshly criticized. Since the Edinburgh missionary conference of 1910, the churches of the third world have vigorously challenged all the "isms" to which Christianity has afforded passage. At the Madras conference in 1938 one delegate declared: "We, the members of the young churches, have no need of your *damnations,* I mean *denominations*". In 1943 the Archbishop of Canterbury William Temple said: "What is needed is that each of our existing Christian denominations should die in order to rise again in a more splendid form." At the youth conference in Lausanne in 1960, Reformed theologian Johannes Hoekendijk took up the same theme: "There will be no unity until we are ready to die as a Reformed, Lutheran, Orthodox in the expectant hope of a resurrection in the presence of Christ, and his one church."

34. Thus confessional identity, even more than ecclesial identity, seems to be mixed. It is a complex of very positive elements and of others that are really negative and marked by sin. In extreme instances, absolutizing the latter features may

extend to a contradiction of Christian identity. We know the temptation in some French circles at the beginning of this century which could be summed up in the formula "just because we are Catholics does not necessarily mean we are Christians".[10] We may think too of certain socio-political confrontations (Northern Ireland, for example) where confessional identity is used as a powerful emotive lever at the risk of ending up by quite simply contradicting Christian identity and gospel love.

35. Confessional identity must be Christian identity: as such it remains faithful to its truth only in so far as it converts constantly to the gospel. This conversion to the gospel must first of all affect each person's own way of understanding the gospel and living it out. It is also an invitation to take up a different stance towards other confessional groups: not to condemn them, but to treat them as brothers and sisters, to hope for them and in them, to seek mutual understanding, peace and full communion.

This does not mean an insipid irenicism, for one of the gospel's requirements for Christian fraternity is for fraternal correction (cf. Matt. 18:15).

III. CHRISTIAN, ECCLESIAL AND CONFESSIONAL CONVERSION

36. In its previous documents the Groupe des Dombes, since 1969, has grouped these three conversions under the term *metanoia*.

In 1976 the document on *The Episcopal Ministry* pointed out that *metanoia* is "a New Testament term currently translated by 'conversion' or 'repentance'. We use it to indicate a change affecting not just interior dispositions and personal behaviour, but also the manner in which ecclesial institutions function, and even, if necessary, their structure".[11]

37. The commentary in the document of 1971, *Towards a Common Eucharistic Faith*, already noted in this regard that:

> This is for us... a step that is at once difficult, demanding and hazardous:

— difficult, because it goes against our natural tendency to defend and justify our own church in any doctrinal discussion;
— demanding, because it is called for by the Holy Spirit and at the same time in full solidarity with our respective churches;
— hazardous, lastly, like every act of faith, which can never escape the snares of the devil, who is always clever at distorting into more or less masochistic and sterile self-criticism what needs to remain a vigilant combat fought in faith and a plea for mercy fraught with hope.[12]

38. In our documents prior to 1985 we still did not distinguish clearly between *ecclesial* conversion and *confessional* conversion. It now seems necessary to deal with three types of conversion: Christian conversion, ecclesial conversion and confessional conversion. This will be the aim of the following analyses.

a) Christian conversion

39. Christian identity rests on a basic conversion: "The kingdom of God has come near; repent, and believe in the good news" (Mark 1:15). This conversion is required by the coming and the resurrection of Jesus Christ. Its absolute nature opens onto a process which is never accomplished fully in this world. This conversion to faith is initiated and celebrated in baptism. Thus it includes an "already there" but also a "not yet". It is a grace which opens onto a task. It leads into an existence which must undergo a continual conversion. That conversion is a struggle conducted in grace against all forms of sin, personal and collective. It is celebrated in the proclamation of the word, and in the sacramental act of reconciliation, as it likewise is in the sacrament of the eucharist.

40. Conversion can take on very diverse forms: a sudden intervention of something new and unheard-of, a slow and continuous progression, the crossing of a series of thresholds. It directly concerns the personality of each believer who is becoming what he or she already is.

b) Ecclesial conversion

41. Ecclesial conversion has the same content as Christian conversion but it concerns church members whether collec-

tively or as an institution, as members of the same communion of faith and sharing certain sinful attitudes. Ecclesial conversion is the constant effort of the church community as such to strive towards its Christian identity.

42. This effort of the *ecclesia semper reformanda* can experience some moments of decisive significance — *kairoi*. The history of the church has known some of these moments, even if they have not been free from excesses; among them, monasticism in the ancient church, movements for reform in the middle ages, the Protestant and Catholic reformations in the sixteenth century, different "awakenings" or revivals emerging from the Reformation churches in the nineteenth century, the profession of faith of the *Bekennendekirche* ("Confessing church") at Barmen in 1934, the *aggiornamento* or "renewal" desired at Vatican II by John XXIII.

43. Ecclesial conversion is a constituent element of ecclesial identity. When fully and universally achieved, each confessional group will be the church in full recognition of the ecclesial character of the others. There will no longer be partial, incomplete ecclesiality for any, either in its own environment or in that of the others. In particular that means the achievement and recognition of the identity of the church's "structure" in all the confessions. This therefore presupposes general doctrinal agreement on the "structure" of the church (as distinct from the different "organizations", but underlying them and realized in them).[13]

44. This effort at conversion is experienced today in churches which are still confessionally divided. It therefore calls for the effort of confessional conversion which constitutes one aspect of it. Just as certainly we can imagine the churches helping each other in a common struggle against all the forms of sin that affect them all in their manner of bearing witness to the gospel.[14]

c) Confessional conversion

45. Confessional conversion relates to the specifically ecumenical efforts achieved by the still-divided churches in trying

to regain full communion. It thus represents a particular aspect of ecclesial conversion in the situation of division.

46. Our confessional identities are an inheritance within which we have to apply a discernment based on the gospel in order to gather together all the positive values in the support of the rich diversity of forms in the church and abandon their sinful dimension. They have to be converted. How could our converted identities — which still contain legitimate diversities — *not* lead us to full communion? For confessional identities become a gracious gift from God for the whole church from the moment they enter the common quest for a fullness of truth and faithfulness that transcends them all.

47. All conversions go through the stage of confessing guilt. Our confessions have to "make confession", to move forward to admitting their limitations and inadequacies, even sins. Each confessional family has to acknowledge that there are elements of Christian tradition which it is incapable, at least for the moment, of receiving and incorporating into its own existence.

48. Confessional conversion for its part too is a constituent element of real confessional identity. This requirement of conversion is therefore an invitation to our confessional identities to open up to each other and let themselves be penetrated by the values which the others bear. In particular, each confession must ask itself if its judgment of the others is really founded on the gospel.

49. This presupposes that each confession will acknowledge that there is in itself matter for conversion, for genuine progress in faithfulness to its Christian and ecclesial identity, whether in the sphere of the language of faith or ecclesial structure or in the existential implementation of Christian reality. These conversions will not be symmetrical, because the deficiencies which affect the different churches are not the same.

50. No conversion can be pre-programmed. While it is urgent that each Christian confession should hear this call to conversion, the conversion itself will come unexpectedly. In the strict sense of the term there is no self-conversion; we receive conversion as a grace.

51. Confessional conversion is first of all conversion to the God of Jesus Christ and consequently a fraternal reconciliation among the churches as they seek full communion and full mutual ecclesial recognition — not to the detriment of confessional identity, but for purification and deepening in line with the gospel.

52. It is along this line that the Groupe des Dombes, in all its documents, has sought to speak about confessional conversion (which it has sometimes also called ecclesial conversion).[15]

d) Balance-sheet

53. We firmly believe that we can speak of identity and conversion only within a clearly stated linguistic convention. We therefore now summarize the terms we are using.

54. By *Christian identity* we mean one's belonging to Christ which is founded on the gift of baptism and lived out with a faith nourished by the word of God, the word that is proclaimed and the eucharistic word. This belonging equally concerns each individual and the church as the people of God.

By *ecclesial identity* we mean the belonging or participation of an individual or of a confessional church in the one, holy, "catholic"[16] and apostolic church.

By *confessional identity* we mean belonging to a confessional church that comes from a specific cultural and historical context, containing its own spiritual and doctrinal profile which distinguishes it from other churches.

55. By *Christian conversion* we mean the response of faith to the call that comes to us from God through Christ. This response takes place in a movement [or process] of constant conversion.

By *ecclesial conversion* we mean the effort required from the whole church and from all the churches for them to be renewed and become more capable of fulfilling their mission in accordance with the motto *ecclesia semper reformanda*.

By *confessional conversion* we understand the ecumenical effort by which a Christian confession cleanses and enriches its own inheritance with the aim of rediscovering full communion with other confessions.

Part II
Examples from History

INTRODUCTION

56. To advance our reflection it seemed good to collect historical evidence. This cannot be a matter of going systematically through history, but of taking soundings from some particularly significant records. We shall consider certain notable instances where we see identities being affirmed and efforts at conversion lived out in very diverse situations. Among these conversions some have been successful experiments which have proved fruitful for the unity of the church. Others have produced mixed effects, leaving a gap between the initial project and its reception. Still others, just because of the ambiguities that governed them, have kept alive or even increased the lack of understanding between churches. Whatever the outcome of each of them, these events are for us a mine of learning material, provided they are subjected to a discriminating analysis that is as close to the gospel as possible.

We shall also collect the testimony of certain great church leaders whose experience may be regarded as typical today. Finally we shall show how certain themes in the church's reflections on doctrine, from antiquity on to our own day, give rise to a "converted" reinterpretation.

I. THE ANCIENT CHURCH AND THE MEDIEVAL CHURCH

a) Three examples of conversion *(metanoia)* in the ancient church (fourth-fifth centuries)

57. Shortly after the Council of Nicea (325), difficult discussions led Athanasius of Alexandria to recognize as being

within the faith of the church those who were uncertain about using a word that was not in scripture (*homoousios* — consubstantial) to refer to the full divinity of Christ. This was to let it be understood that the ecumenical council had not gone beyond the scriptural evidence to canonize its own terminology.

58. A few decades later, between 370 and 379, Basil of Caesarea was bold enough to defend the divinity of the Holy Spirit but without saying that the Holy Spirit was God. In so doing he judged that abruptly to proclaim the divinity of the Spirit risked dividing the church and thus grieving the Paraclete himself. It was necessary to avoid the catastrophe of a profession of faith that would end up dividing the church.[17]

59. Following the Council of Ephesus (431), Cyril of Alexandria, realizing that his attitudes had led to a general excommunication, did not hesitate to recognize as perfectly orthodox a theological expression of faith in Christ — that of the bishops of the region of Antioch — to which he had till then turned a deaf ear, thus clearing of any suspicion of heresy their remarkable insistence on the man Jesus in whom the word dwells as in its temple.[18]

60. Perhaps it needed centuries for the churches to appreciate these three spiritual, theological and pastoral acts. At all events, encounters of church leaders in the last few years have turned them to good account. Thus, to show just how far one had to go in making sacrifices for the unity of Christians, Paul VI affirmed in dialogue with Athenagoras I on 25 July 1967 that

> love must help us as it helped Hilary and Athanasius to recognize the identity of faith beyond the differences of vocabulary when serious divergences were dividing the Christian episcopate. Did not St Basil himself in his pastoral love defend the true faith in the Holy Spirit by avoiding the use of certain words which, however exact they might be, could turn out to be a stumbling-block for part of the Christian people? And did not St Cyril of Alexandria in 433 agree to set aside the fine theology that was his in order to make peace with John of Antioch, after he was sure that, beyond the different expressions, their faith was identical?[19]

61. The pope's final sentence was echoed on 20 June 1989 by Metropolitan Damaskinos of Switzerland addressing the Coptic Patriarch of Alexandria, Shenouda III, in the commission for dialogue between the Orthodox church and the pre-Chalcedonian Oriental churches:

> You have referred to the theology — which we share — of Cyril of Alexandria regarding "one nature of God the Incarnate Word". Our desire and prayer is that his humility and high sense of responsibility may be an example to us. For he did not insist on the priority of his own theology — admirable as it was — in the hope of reconciling himself with John of Antioch in 433, after he had been convinced that, beyond the differences, their faith was the same.[20]

62. These three examples represent an astonishing conversion *(metanoia)*. Besides the fact that they concern bishops whose purpose was the commitment of their community and the communion of the churches, and that what was at issue was the actual expression of the faith in theology and not the kind of free and non-threatening questions raised by a Gregory of Nazianzus,[21] we are in the presence here of the very rule of faith, its solemn credal expression and its apostolic foundation. What was explicitly at issue in these three instances was the Nicene faith — in the first and third cases the very way in which its terminology about Christ was understood, and in the second the appropriate way of understanding faith in the Spirit.

63. What we are saying is that the church, in its quest for unity, must be open to a renunciation which is not a desertion or a denial or a betrayal but does not limit itself to sacrificing prejudices, habits or strong emotions. One would have to speak of a conversion of the spirit and not only of the heart. To understand that the theology by which the confessional church to which we belong is not the only one capable of expressing the Christian mystery, even on essentials (Cyril); to know how to be silent or rather how to say what is essential at the appropriate moment, even if not explicitly, so that unity may be upheld or created (Basil); to say that even the best and most carefully chosen words must be the objects of understanding,

not veneration, and that they are subject to variation and must therefore be translated both into other languages and into other terminology (Hilary and Athanasius): such would be the conversion of the churches today if they wish to be faithful to the faith in its earliest stages.

b) The "conversions" of St Augustine (354-430)

64. In tackling Augustine's spiritual pilgrimage we are changing the ground a bit. Here it is no longer a matter of ecclesial conversions and decisions but of the personal development of a human being. However, the career of Augustine takes on an ecclesial value, and in the Western church it constituted an exemplary point of reference (even if it included some shadowy elements). In fact, Augustine initiated a new way of undergoing the conversions to which the Christian faith invites us. We shall find these aspects also in many other witnesses of Christianity, especially Luther.

65. The spiritual pilgrimage which led Augustine from unbelief to faith (and we do indeed say from unbelief to faith, not from paganism to the church) is a *conversion to God and to the Christ* of orthodoxy.[22] We see him, a young schoolboy at Madaura, gradually distancing himself from the faith of his early childhood. We find him again at Tagaste where his year of idleness does not guide him towards God. At Carthage he leads the life of a student for whom spiritual questions hardly arise.

Suddenly he finds philosophy in reading Cicero's *Hortensius*. In it he discovers the vanity of human success and the fundamental importance of the quest for wisdom. "But this book altered my affections, and turned my prayers to Thyself, O Lord; and made me have other purposes and desires... and I... began now to arise, that I might return to Thee."[23]

66. That search for God was to continue through Manicheism, the encounter with Neoplatonism and the preaching of Ambrose. Then Augustine discovered scripture and the meekness of Christ the mediator who is able to free him from the weight of his sin. Gradually his intellectual doubts dissolve, and he comes to the well-known scene in the Milan garden where his conversion crystallizes. Through a passage of the

apostle Paul (Rom. 13:13ff.) he sees the last obstacles fall away. Having become free in order to live in chastity he converted to the God revealed in scripture: "For Thou convertedst me unto Thyself, so that I sought neither wife, nor any hope of this world, standing in that rule of faith..."[24]

But Augustine did not leave it at that. At Cassiciacum he led the studious life of a monk. His writings from that period reveal his state of mind: first and foremost he is a philosopher, but a Christian philosopher. His conversion to the God of Jesus Christ was consolidated, as the *Soliloquia* testify.

67. When we look at this pilgrimage we see that first of all it was a conversion to God: this is the dominant feature of that period in Augustine's life: "And Thou surpassingly art the Selfsame, Who *art not changed*; and in Thee is rest which forgetteth all toil, for there is none other with Thee, nor are we to seek those many other things which are not what Thou art: but Thou, Lord, *alone* hast *made me dwell in hope.*"[25] There too, however, we find an ecclesial aspect of conversion. The church is present through Monica and the education she has given her son, through the Christian community which intervenes to try to bring Augustine back to the faith, through Ambrose and his preaching, through the meeting with Victorinus. This conversion to God is accompanied *sotto voce* by the motif of a conversion to the catholic and universal church.

68. Moreover, when Augustine was converted, it was not only to the catholic church in the sense of universal, but also to the catholic church in the sense of orthodox. "But somewhat later, I confess, did I learn, how in that saying, *The word was made flesh,* the Catholic Truth is distinguished from the falsehood of Photinus. For the rejection of heretics makes the tenets of Thy Church and sound doctrine to stand out more clearly."[26] In this way the confessional aspect is certainly present in Augustine's pilgrimage, not primarily in the form of a "confessional conversion" as defined earlier, but rather in the form of conversion to orthodoxy. Thus in this first part of Augustine's life, which led him to baptism in Milan in 387, conversion to God, to the church and to orthodoxy overlap, but with conversion to the God of Jesus Christ predominating:

"So I was confounded, and converted: and I joyed, O my God, that the One Only Church, the body of Thine Only Son (wherein the name of Christ had been put upon me as an infant), had no taste for infantile conceits..."[27]

69. The second part of Augustine's life, leading from his baptism to the episcopate, is very specially the time of his conversion to the church. That conversion begins with baptism which brings him into the church. Back in Tagaste in Africa, he lives in community with his friends, this time in a genuinely Christian community. He is increasingly interested in ecclesiastical questions: he is called by the people of God to the priesthood and begins his ministry in the congregation of Hippo. His activities and his theological reflection then give him the opportunity to stress the need for an *ecclesial conversion*.

70. A third period in Augustine's life, that of his episcopate, is marked more by his conversion to orthodoxy. One need only think of the struggles against Donatism and Pelagianism. But the aspect of *confessional conversion* also appears in this same context. In telling the faithful of the "catholic" church that the Donatists are their brothers and that their baptism is that of Christ, Augustine is a genuine ancestor of the conversion of the churches to Christian unity. When he tells Pelagius that by crowning our merits God is crowning his own gifts, Augustine is indicating to the whole church that in its essence it derives from that good pleasure of God which is called mercy.

71. Nevertheless we can trace in this period the presence of two other conversions. *The City of God* is the best witness to that persistence of conversion to God and ecclesial conversion. Augustine opposes polytheism and reaffirms the monotheism of the biblical revelation. In face of the community's perturbation about the future he affirms the enduring nature of the City of God which continues through the ages to arrive at the kingdom. This time again the three motifs are mixed and interwoven, even if conversion to orthodox catholicity takes first place: "So why, O heretic, do you set aside the question to be debated in order to attack a man?... Am I the Catholic

Church?... It is enough that I am in it... the church known throughout the whole universe is to be found where I was baptized."[28]

72. We draw a double lesson from Augustine's pilgrimage. On the one hand it was the conversion of the church that enabled him to say: "Thou madest us for thyself, and our heart is restless, until it repose in Thee."[29] Augustine was converted thanks to a bishop who was faithful to the Nicene faith, in a church renewed by the preaching of the word. "...Thy wonderful works most fully attested,... wrought in the true faith and the Church Catholic."[30]

Let us remember on the other hand that his personal conversions gave rise to a dynamic of renewal for the ancient churches of the East and the West[31] and exercised a crucial influence on the Latin church of the following centuries, and especially on the Protestant Reformers. One could even say of him, fittingly enough, that — like the empire of Charlemagne — he had been somewhat partitioned by his heirs!

c) Identity without conversion: theocratic hardening and the breach between East and West (ninth-fourteenth centuries)

73. From the ninth to the fourteenth century the assertion of the confessional identities of the East and West increased continually and hardened into differentiation. On each side withdrawal into its own identity and the polemical atmosphere finally called in question the ecclesial character of the other, despite the continuance of many acts of communion and certain sincere quests for unity. In this context evidences of concern for conversion are few in number, fragile and casual.

74. Both theologically and politically the Gregorian reform at the close of the eleventh century consolidated the Roman identity and its claim to ecclesial primacy. Stimulated by the reforming monastic orders of the twelfth century (for example, that of Bernard de Clairvaux) the reform remedied the anarchy of feudal pluralism in Western Christendom, attacked corrupt *mores* among the clergy and freed the churches from dependence on the temporal power of the princes. But it did not put

an end to the ambiguity represented by the temporal power of the papacy, and its effect was the development of an increasingly authoritarian Roman centralism.

75. The result was the excessive politicizing of the Roman hierarchy and the infiltration of the people of God by streams of lay piety which genuinely cared about reform but were increasingly uncontrolled. The requirement of theocratic uniformity meant that some of these lay movements were rejected by the Roman identity (such as the Waldensians of Lyons and the Lollards in England), others were tolerated (such as the Beguines) or brought into line (like the Franciscan movement, which however lost its lay character).

76. With the evolution of papal authority the Latin church entered the path of legalism and clericalization. Its confrontations with temporal powers led it to see itself too as a power. The papacy was seen as one power alongside the others. The ecclesiology of a vertical catholicity prevailed over that of a horizontal catholicity of the whole Christian people, clergy and laity. The awareness of unity, far from being consolidated by this development, lost what little confidence it had gained in the high middle ages under the efforts of the preaching monks.

77. The rift between Rome and Constantinople in 1054 — prepared for by a slow, mutual drifting apart of East and West, and aggravated by the excesses of certain crusades — was one of the effects of the Roman claim to a form of ecclesial primacy which was envisaged as a direct authoritarian government of the whole church. Rome affirmed its own identity in an exclusive and intransigent manner; it succumbed to the temptation to make the Roman sacramental obedience the unique and decisive criterion for belonging to the church. Sometimes it seemed that everything was as it should be in the East except obedience to the Roman church; sometimes Rome seemed to think that the Eastern church, separated from it, was no longer the church.[32]

78. The authority of the Roman pontiff was asserted as the principle for the church as the body of Christ. Monarchical in its nature, the Roman identity defined itself as the head, the mother, the pivot, the fountainhead, the foundation of every

church. At the beginning of the thirteenth century the bishop of Rome, having been the "vicar of Peter", became the "vicar of Christ". No local congregation could find its ecclesial identity save in relation to the Roman identity because of the institution [of the church] made in the person of Peter.[33] Later attempts at reconciliation, such as those at Lyons in 1274 and in Florence in 1439, failed because of the atmosphere thus created between the churches of the East and of the West.

79. In this situation of a breakdown in relations, voices were nevertheless raised in favour of a conversion of the medieval church. In the fourteenth century the desertion of the episcopal see at Rome in the period of the Avignon popes and the struggle between two or even three popes at the time of the great Western schism raised doubts about the genuine ecclesiality of the Roman identity. Great mystics like Mechthild of Magdeburg (ca. 1207/1210-1282/1294), Meister Eckhart (ca. 1260-1327) and Catherine of Siena (ca. 1347-1380) called the papacy and the whole people of the church to ecclesial conversion. Anti-authoritarian ecclesiologies like those of John Wycliffe (ca. 1330-1384) and Jan Hus (1370-1415) called for such a conversion in reaction against the Roman confessional identity. The question of reform (*causa reformationis*) became a conciliar matter but was constantly put off during the whole fifteenth century and neutralized by the continual rivalry between the authority of the pope and the authority of councils.

80. The church at the close of the middle ages became immobilized in that struggle, in which the claims of the Roman identity paralyzed every effort at genuine ecclesial conversion. Bogged down in the abuses of its clergy, incapable of adequately meeting the spiritual needs of *devotio moderna* — which emphasized divine initiative, individual piety and withdrawal from the world — and concerned to protect its political powers, the Roman church built up internal tensions which were to undermine its unity a century later. Incapable of calling its confessional identity in question, it could no longer prevent the break-up of Western Christendom into separate, diverging churches.

81. Confronted with these new forms of Christianity in the West, the churches of the Byzantine empire, aware of their continuance in Orthodoxy, seem not to have questioned their own identity with the church of the time of the apostles and the fathers. They retained the pride of being the first churches, since the gospel was written in their language and they had welcomed the Saviour's message earlier than the others. Hence their lack of interest in and suspicion of what was happening in the world of the so-called holy Roman empire and the realms of the barbarians.

82. In the East the major problem was still to protect the Byzantine empire, where the emperor played an eminent role in the life of the church. Since Constantine, the fate of the church and of the empire were linked *de facto* and *de jure*. Their relations were understood in terms of the theory of the "symphony [harmony] of temporal and spiritual power" — contrary to the Western theory of the "two swords". Such a situation, extending through the centuries, kept alive the confusions between the two spheres, and continued to contribute to a certain historical immobility and withdrawal into their own identity.

83. For instance, while the origins of the iconoclastic heresy did indeed have a religious basis, its consequences were as political as they were religious. It was as much a state matter as a church matter. In these circumstances religious "reform" depended as much on the emperor as on the patriarch, if not more. Here the reform was always already effected, but unlike the Western reforms, it was made directly at the top by the emperor together with the patriarch. An identity without fissure was consolidated, but it did not open itself up to conversion.

84. Moreover, the ecclesiology of communion, unilaterally understood, was so perfectly orthodox as to be unassailable but it became so abstract that it no longer had much to do with reality. A gulf was created between the vagaries of history and the theology that was enunciated. The great danger of this state of affairs is to shut oneself up in a theology that is so perfect at the level of language that it makes the idea of ecclesial and

confessional conversion difficult. But this rejection of conversion now contradicts the great Orthodox tradition itself, which has always stressed the solidarity of orthodoxy and orthopraxis.

85. Our reading of these five centuries may seem harsh. Of course that period is not limited to what we have said about it. There were a number of personal conversions, and movements of evangelism and spirituality blossomed, especially the Franciscans and Dominicans in the West and hesychasm in the East. Church institutions as such, however, lacked an attitude of conversion during this period. Consequently the best efforts of conversion were condemned to be bogged down. The continual deterioration of the situation was responsible for the explosions and divisions of the sixteenth century.

d) Balance-sheet

86. The history of the ancient and medieval church enables us to verify the functioning of the categories of *Christian, ecclesial and confessional* conversion and identity which were identified, and distinguished from each other, in the section entitled "Clues for a Terminology". It testifies to genuine conversion experiences that can inspire us even today. It also reveals that in some instances a hardening in relation to identity clearly hindered or excluded the fundamental movement of conversion.

87. The various types of conversion may appear simultaneously and they then bear witness fully to conversion in terms of the gospel. Often, too, one of the three dimensions has a dominant position for a time, but in such a way that the two other dimensions are also present and discernible.

II. THE CHURCH AT THE BEGINNING OF THE MODERN AGE

a) The Protestant Reformation

Two calls for ecclesial conversion

88. In his spiritual pilgrimage, the vigour of his theological thought and the passion of his reforming activity, Martin

Luther (1483-1546) incontestably represents an essential element in this great movement for conversion which appeared in the sixteenth century. He underwent "a crucial experience, a sudden illumination, a liberating discovery, a new understanding of the righteousness of God".[34] The debate which set him in opposition to the Roman authority and led to his excommunication related to fundamental problems of the faith like justification; but in the light of recent historiography one may wonder whether "the real breach is located in relation not to soteriology but to ecclesiology".[35] The ecclesiological consequences of Luther's challenge were not slow to appear, as the great treatises of 1520 attest (cf. "Address to the Christian Nobility of the German Nation" or "A Prelude Concerning the Babylonian Captivity of the Church").

Caught in that tension between the demands of the gospel on the one hand and his concern for the church and its authority on the other, Luther dedicated his "Freedom of a Christian" to Pope Leo X in October 1520, addressing an urgent appeal to him for ecclesial conversion:

> I have... turned my heart away from Your Holiness so little that I have constantly formed all the best of wishes for you and for your Holy See. With what zeal have I not prayed for that and with what groans have I not asked God for them to be granted!... In fact, allow me to tell you straightforwardly that I am not aware of having spoken of you other than in the most exalted and best of terms on every occasion when I have had to mention you. If I had acted otherwise I could only thoroughly disapprove of myself.... It is true that your fame... is too renowned and august, not to mention your life, which is without blemish, to be called in question in any way and by anyone, even the most highly placed....
> On the other hand, I have constantly and violently attacked impious doctrines and have been not a little scathing towards my opponents, not because of their bad behaviour but because of their impiety (their opposition to the gospel).... For the rest, I have not entered into argument with anyone regarding their conduct. It is simply a question of the word of truth. On any other point I am happy to yield to anyone you wish, but the word I neither can nor desire to renounce or deny.... There is no one for whom that is not

clearer than daylight: the Roman church, formerly holy among all the churches, has become a den of thieves, overflowing with licence, a house in which debauchery flaunts itself more than anywhere else.... Is it not true that under our vast heavens there is nothing more corrupt, more pestilential or abhorrent than the Roman Curia?... I was so far removed from anger against your person that I hoped to win your favour and stand by your side for your salvation by attacking your prison, not to say your hell, with all my strength.... Moreover, I cannot tolerate that the word of God should be subjected to the laws of our interpretations, for what matters is that the word should not be bound — the word which teaches in perfect freedom.... Beware, therefore, Leo, my Father, of paying heed to the sirens who make you something more than an ordinary man — almost a god..., you are the servant of those who serve and no one in the world is in a more pitiable and dangerous situation. Do not let yourself be seduced by those who make you the master of the world and who do not allow that anyone can be a Christian without your approval.... Those who recognize the interpretation of scripture as being solely your responsibility are in error. They are only seeking to install all their impieties in the church under the guarantee of your name.[36]

89. Echoing that appeal by Luther is another one, equally urgent, which came from Pope Adrian VI, successor of Leo X. The statement he told his legate Chieregati to make to the delegates of the imperial Diet meeting in Nuremberg in 1523 is inspired by the same concern for ecclesial conversion:

> We freely acknowledge that God has permitted this persecution of the church because of human sins, and especially those of the priests and prelates; for it is certain that the hand of God is not shortened, that he could save us, but that sin separates us from him and prevents him from listening to us. Holy scripture teaches us throughout that the faults of the people have their origin in the faults of the clergy.... We know that, even in the Holy See, for years many abominations were committed: abuse of holy things, transgression of the commandments, so that everything has become a scandal. We need not wonder that sickness has come down from the heads to the members, from the popes to the prelates. All of us, prelates and clerics, have turned aside from the path of righteousness. It is long enough since anyone has done what is good; this is why we must all glorify God and humble

ourselves before him; each of us must examine how he has fallen, and examine himself more strictly than God will examine him in the day of his wrath. Consequently... we shall devote ourselves wholly to making a start by improving the Roman Curia from which all the evil has perhaps come; from it will come the cure, as from it came the sickness. We consider ourselves committed all the more to do so as the whole world is hungry for such a reform.[37]

Ecclesial identity and the emergence of the confessional churches
90. The appeals of Luther and Adrian VI, issued in the early years of the divisive sixteenth-century reforms, fell on deaf ears. From 1530 — when the Protestants were obliged by the emperor to submit confessions of faith to the diet of Augsburg — interchurch dialogue on unity foundered on the question of confessional identity. This was affirmed and defended on the Protestant side, as if ecclesial conversion must necessarily take the form of adherence by the entire Western church to the identity set forth by the Protestant Reformation in its confessions of faith. This is illustrated, for instance, in the church of Strasbourg which, having changed to Reformation worship in 1529, demanded four years later that every citizen should adhere to the confession of faith adopted by the city. Of the three types of conversion — Christian, ecclesial and confessional — it was the third which became the criterion for the other two.

91. Nevertheless, at the very period of the Protestant Reformation there were consultations on unity — notably in 1540-41 at Hagenau, Worms and Regensburg — in an attempt to prevent the Western church, which was organically one, from breaking up into mutually hostile confessional churches. These colloquies took place at the instigation not of the church authorities but of Emperor Charles V. Both the Roman authorities and those of the newly reformed communities sought to oppose these discussions on unity. In fact, Charles V, against the advice of both the pope and Luther, wanted to test the possibility of subjecting confessional identities, which were tending to gain the upper hand, to an effort at reconversion to ecclesial unity. There were some political motives for

restoring pre-eminence to ecclesial identity over the emerging plurality of confessional churches. This ecclesiastical policy of Charles V was a failure. The dynamic that fostered confessional pluralism plunged into crisis the principle of Christendom epitomized by the *corpus christianum*. The decline of the awareness of Christendom was at once the cause and the effect of the emergence of hostile confessional pluralism.

92. In this new situation of the church, the Protestant Reformers emphasized in their ecclesiology the distinction — but not the separation — between the church invisible (the church as the body of Christ) and the visible church (the human institution). The former was seen as the real ecclesial community in Christ, which was known to him alone; the latter as the organized, established community of Christians. It was possible to belong to the one without necessarily belonging to the other. This distinction made it possible to deny the church in the Roman obedience the genuineness of its ecclesial identity and its claim to be the one church. The "papistical" church of the medieval period was denounced in its organic and historical reality as the false church, the church of the antichrist. The church of the Protestant Reformation could thus justify its own claim to full ecclesial status despite the breach initiated by the excommunications that came from the traditional church.[38]

93. The Protestant Reformers credited the church they had reformed with full ecclesial identity. When they claimed this for their churches alone, expecting that the whole Western church would reform itself according to the same criteria, the dialogue on unity became sterile, for the Roman church did the same over against them. Nevertheless, this claim to be fully the church compelled the Protestant reformers who laid special stress on ecclesiology — such as Martin Bucer, Philip Melanchthon and John Calvin — to return emphatically to the "marks" of genuine ecclesiality: unity, holiness, catholicity and apostolicity. Thus distancing themselves from spiritualizing tendencies, they were compelled to set up new ecclesial institutions corresponding to the theological standards of their confessions of faith.[39]

94. These same Reformers entered into dialogue with the theologians of the Roman church. We find them at the colloquies on unity of 1540-1541. For the Protestant Reformers there could not be several churches of Jesus Christ; however, differences of opinion and practice were possible without the unity of the faith being broken.[40] Thus they affirmed that unity of ecclesial identity was possible in confessional pluralism.

Luther, Bucer and Melanchthon recognized in the Roman church of their day, and of previous centuries, its share of ecclesiality even at the worst moments of the medieval abuses. Nevertheless, neither the churches that emerged from the Protestant Reformation nor the Roman church were able alone to claim to be the church in its fullness. Conversion of their ecclesial identity was becoming necessary for each of the churches that had become confessional churches, including the Roman church, if it did not wish its ecclesial identity to lose the "mark" of unity. Nevertheless, and despite this openness to unity, these Protestant Reformers were convinced that the conversion of the whole church (Roman and Protestant) to ecclesial identity would lead it to the fundamental principles propounded by them.[41]

95. The Protestant Reformers, and after them the Protestant theologians who were concerned about unity, called for a general council as a final court of appeal and authoritative doctrinal guide on unity.[42] They saw in such a body a possibility to rediscover the ecclesial unity which was in process of breaking up. Thus their ecclesiology fell into the conciliarist line of the fifteenth and sixteenth centuries. Their ecclesiological motives, however, came up against the opposition of the popes of their day and were blocked by the political motives of Charles V, who also called for such a council. The failure to convene such a council at the beginning of the Protestant reforming movement destroyed the chances for a conversion of the church to unity at the Council of Trent.

b) The Catholic reform

96. The Catholic reform[43] was not a *creatio ex nihilo*. In recent years historians have clearly shown that the reforms of

the sixteenth century had been preceded by many spiritual currents, such as *devotio moderna*. Moreover, the Catholic reformation in the proper sense of the term is not reducible to the dogmatic texts of the Council of Trent (1545-63). The disciplinary decrees for the reform of the clergy had a crucial influence and were the channel for a spiritual current which stemmed from a genuinely mystical inspiration.[44]

97. Another caveat is also essential: the Council of Trent should not be confused with Tridentinism.[45] The Council was a reaction, often over-sensitive though well-considered, within a Western church which was becoming aware of a division whose effects it had not yet evaluated. Tridentinism, by contrast, was both a systematic organization of doctrine carried out on the basis of the council's documents, regarded as almost self-sufficient, and the establishment of institutions which would leave a considerable mark on Roman Catholicism.

98. *Mutatis mutandis* the Catholic reformation was to experience the same problem as the Protestant Reformation. Just as the Protestant "confessions" drifted into confessionalism, so, too, the heritage of Trent degenerated into Tridentinism, with the risk of some potential unfaithfulness to that heritage. The danger was that of confusing a stage on the road with the entire journey.

Christian identity and Christian conversion

99. If it is not too pretentious to make an overall judgment on the Council of Trent from the standpoint of Christian identity, it may be thought that we find there a kind of "recentring" in Christ, the source and cause of salvation. Whether the issue is the sacraments, the sources of revelation (scripture and Tradition) or justification and sanctification, we may expect to see a magnification of the work of divine grace. At all events the theses of Trent could not take away from the primacy and gratuitousness of the gift of God. We are thus confronted with a Christological theocentrism, which certainly leaves little room for the Holy Spirit. Following a certain Thomist inspiration, linked to a pastoral

concern for the transformation of Christians, the Council affirms that the individual must cooperate with God in the process of justification and sanctification. That cooperation may be demanded by God because it is given by his grace. The primary initiative is wholly God's, while human beings are given the initiative of letting themselves be transformed by him.

100. From that starting-point it is possible to state that the Council of Trent, especially in its first period (1546-47), wanted a more spiritual church, a less ritualistic and less legalistic Christianity, which would allow the believer to enter more fully into the mystery of salvation. The text on the catechumen's progess to baptism, in the decree on justification, is all the more exemplary in this respect, coming as it does from a period which hardly knew anything but infant baptism.[46]

We may thus speak positively of Christian conversion at the Council of Trent, a conversion which affected not only the moral behaviour of church members but also their profound adherence to the mystery of the faith.

101. It remains true that doctrinally this conversion also had negative effects. For, in so far as the true interpretation of the gospel is at stake, Trent, in reaction to the Protestant Reformation, over-emphasized the institutional church. This subsequently caused some confusion between obedience to the faith and submission to the authorities. A typical Roman Catholic dogmatic sensitivity began to develop, leading by a consistent logic to Vatican I.

Ecclesial identity and ecclesial conversion

102. The Council of Trent did not consider ecclesiology to be its theme. The reason for this is evident, given the historical context: the Protestant Reformers were basically attacking the doctrine of justification and the sacraments. It might even be said that Trent ignored ecclesiology and was not responsible for the ecclesiology that found its spokesperson in Cardinal Bellarmine, which was a defence and illustration of the church as an institution.[47]

103. In the realm of ecclesiology the Council of Trent appears to be affected by a double handicap:

— *A deficiency:* it says nothing about the church as a mystery. It was necessary to await the twentieth century and Vatican II for the mystical current in ecclesiology to resurface in official documents. The Christocentric ecclesiology of the Epistle to the Ephesians does not shine through in the work of Trent. Likewise, we are far removed from the ecclesiology of the Greek fathers, in which the Logos sanctifies a united and regenerated human nature.

104. — *A superfluity:* by this we mean a view according to which God seems to act "directly" in the church. The council lacked a sense of ecclesial "mediations" through which the mediation of the sole Mediator is in fact disclosed and implemented. The distance between Christ and the church is not pronounced, and still less the distance between the church and the kingdom of God as found in the gospels.

105. What conversion did the Council of Trent cause from the perspective of the church?

On the positive side the church felt more linked to Christ and recognized that it should be more obedient to him. For the church, as the living instrument of Jesus, must not get in his way with practices contrary to the gospel. On this point some isolated voices in the church have been able humbly to ask forgiveness.[48]

106. On the negative side the absence of ecclesiology had the predictable consequence of considerably strengthening the institution as such. Confronted with the Protestants who challenged it, the Council placed such a high value on the institution that it was later virtually equated with the mystery of the church. That equation is all the more regrettable because it linked up with another equation that would mark Catholic theological teaching to a great extent in the following centuries: the identification of Catholic doctrine with the sum of the refutations of Protestant theses at the Council of Trent.[49] But a collection of counter-propositions does not constitute a balanced doctrinal synthesis. "Bellarminism" would not really to be overcome until Vatican II.

Confessional identity and confessional conversion

107. The confessional identity of Catholicism emerged at that time even though Catholic theology had always abhorred the idea of regarding Catholicism as a "confession". Politically it was indeed to be regarded as such. Of course this was more a result than a deliberate choice. But at the start of the Council of Trent Catholics had not yet become aware of the incurable ecclesial division with the Protestants.

108. Subsequently the established church of the period realized it was confronted for the first time with an insurmountable "heretical" problem which was bringing authentic ecclesial bodies into existence. This was something wholly different from the separation from the Eastern church, which had been seen as a "schism". Hence direct opposition to the theses of the Protestant Reformers (often reduced to statements completely divorced from their context, as in the canons pronouncing anathemas) constituted "Catholicism" and gave it a confessional inflexibility. The worldwide spread of this situation, which was still very European, was to take place through the expansion of the Western churches in the Americas, Africa and, in a more limited way, in Asia.

109. While the differences between Protestants and Catholics ought to have retained their specific form, their serious nature and their challenge, it was realized about a century after the Council of Trent that they boiled down to a popular simplification which has had free rein up to our own day. For instance, if the Catholics' confession of faith should normally attest to the real presence of Christ in the eucharist, the role of Mary in the economy of salvation and the pope's ministry of unity, the result is that the Protestant is "identified" as one who does not "believe" in the real presence or the Holy Virgin or the pope.[50] Forgotten are the Protestants' faith in Christ as the one Saviour, their love and knowledge of the word of God and the positive value of the Lord's supper which they celebrate.

The understanding which the Catholic church has of itself is accompanied by an "integralism" that tends to deny that aspects of the Christian faith are obscured or minimized in it.

This simplification is also expressed in the "diptychs": Protestants believe in the word, Catholics in the sacrament; Protestants in scripture, Catholics in the Tradition; Protestants are saved subjectively by faith, Catholics objectively through the efficacy of the sacrament, and so on. Through these caricatures, Catholicism has forged a practical confessional identity in which polemics has extended statements of faith beyond their real meaning and devalued the identity of other Christians.

110. Were there any positive aspects in this identification of confessional type? The impact of the Tridentine conciliar decrees on church discipline, the abundant fruit of the establishment of seminaries, and the mystical and apostolic movement of what was to be called the French school demonstrate beyond any doubt that Catholicism had implemented its reformation. Three points emphasize this: everything relating to catechesis and catechisms (some of which adopted the structure of the Protestant catechisms); the organization of ministerial training for genuine preaching of the word; the obligation laid on bishops and parish priests to be "resident", which means that every pastor must be present with his flock.

111. The negative aspects of this confessional identification are familiar enough. Tridentinism, sometimes going beyond its own intentions, reinforced ecclesiastical centralism; it caused the loss of what was to be valued in a moderate Gallicanism; and finally it brought about a regrettable identification of catholicity with Romanism. Catholicism in the "modern" sense of the term was born, no longer as an essential description of Christianity itself but as one of the great Christian denominations which continued to be separated from each other.

c) From confessions of faith to confessionalism (seventeenth-eighteenth centuries)

112. The Protestant and Catholic reformations, despite their aspects of confessional polemics, were both inspired by the desire for ecclesial conversion. Luther's personal experience may illustrate this: it was sustained by a threefold conversion — Christian, ecclesial and confessional — comparable with

what we set out above in relation to St Augustine. In the historical situations brought about by Luther's movement, however, misunderstandings and rejections led to a distortion of the reforming dynamic. Pre-eminence was given to confessional identity, which became the point of reference for ecclesial identity, the one or the other then serving as the criterion for Christian identity. This inversion of priorities distorted the possibilities of conversion in the two reformations. Each side wanted to lead the entire holy Roman empire or the whole kingdom of France to the same confessional identity, which would be regulative for ecclesial identity. The latter became in turn the ultimate yardstick for the Christian identity of each of its members. The threefold conversion was caught in a trap because any conversion could only end up in one confession or another.

113. The formula *cuius regio eius religio* ("a person's religion is that of his country"),[51] which had been applied since the peace of Augsburg in 1555 and confirmed in the treaties of Westphalia in 1648, illustrates the divisive principle of the territorially confessional churches and the reversal of the priorities among the three conversions. This political principle froze the situation of the confessional churches — and historically the Roman church is to be thought of as such from that moment. Confessional identity, having become a yardstick for ecclesial identity, could no longer be challenged, as each confession regarded itself as the only bearer of the characteristic "marks" of full ecclesiality — of the fullness of the church. An ecclesial conversion could be regarded only as a denial (of one's ecclesiality as a confession), or even as treason.

114. Thus from the end of the sixteenth century until the eighteenth century the encounters of the confessional churches that emerged from the two reformations became confrontations, wars of religion and incurable divisions. The dialogue for unity could only be confined to a few conversations between individuals, always doomed to failure in a climate dominated by controversies.[52]

115. There were nevertheless some encounters, consultations and efforts at unity throughout that period. Thus in

France in the seventeenth century, Gallicanism drove certain Catholic and Protestant theologians to the "unionist" reconciliation, in which unity had to be achieved to Rome's disadvantage. In Germany the Lutheran Georg Callixtus (1586-1656) called for a consensus based on the confessions of faith of the ecumenical councils of the ancient church and the tradition of the fathers. He rejected doctrinal intolerance and commended a more irenical dialogue which would recognize members of the different confessional churches as "true Christians".[53] This effort at unity made itself evident even in the Orthodox church where Patriarch Cyril Lukaris (1572-1638) attempted a reconciliation of Orthodoxy and Calvinism, which proved abortive.[54] In England, to combat the successive persecutions of non-conformist Protestants or Catholics, some Anglican theologians sought to convince the other confessional churches of the need for a "middle way".

116. Following the Thirty Years' War (1618-48), voices were raised in favour of going back to Christian conversion as the priority and yardstick for ecclesial and confessional conversions — in other words, a return to this order of priorities: Christian conversion, ecclesial conversion, confessional conversion. These voices came from movements challenging the divided state of the church: for instance from pietism, through its initiator, the Alsatian Philipp Jakob Spener (1635-1705), or from missionary universalism, through the Czech Jan Amos Comenius (1592-1670).

117. Disappointed at the inability of the confessional churches to find their path of ecclesial conversion towards unity, Protestant theologians like Spener, Comenius and others put forward an ecumenical plan for missionary universalism. This leap beyond confessional particularism was to be a return towards the very meaning of the churches: to be at the service of the whole of humanity. This ecclesial conversion, they thought, would be the new reformation of all the confessional churches. *Reformatio vera in unitatem reducit* — genuine reformation leads back to unity — wrote Comenius.[55] A *reformatio* of this kind would proceed by way of the conversion of theological discussion to the primary mission of the

church.[56] These "irenicals" for unity considered that the reform of the church had not been completed,[57] and that confessional identity was not the end-result but a stage along the way to full and shared ecclesiality.

118. These calls for ecclesial conversion and for restoring the true priority among the three conversions did not succeed in making themselves sufficiently heard. In the eighteenth century and under the influence of the Enlightenment the principle of religious *tolerance*, rather than *unity*, became the criterion for the co-existence, side by side, of the confessional churches. Unity was only restored by the confesssional churches as a "mark" of ecclesial and Christian conversion, from the nineteenth century onwards, under the pressure and fear of materialism and secularism, which made them gradually doubt their respective and separate claims to full and sufficient ecclesiality. That was how the way opened up for the contemporary ecumenical movement.

d) Balance-sheet

119. When the confessional churches, as they were produced historically by the divisive reforms of the sixteenth century, each claim full correspondence between their confessional identity and ecclesial identity, they render their confessional situation inflexible. Faithfulness to ecclesial identity is then inevitably confused with faithfulness to doctrinal formulas and confessional practices. Any ecclesial conversion that challenges confessional inviolability, even on grounds of unity, is then regarded as a denial of ecclesiality itself.

120. Conversion is then limited to individual conversion, the only remaining locus for change. In an historical situation of this kind, only personal Christian identity remains open to a process of transformation.

121. The era of confessionalism, in which the churches equate their confessional identity with full and sufficient ecclesial identity, illustrates the risk which such ecclesiology poses to any possibility of conversion. Turning upside down the priorities among the three conversions causes and consolidates ecclesial division. Confusing confessional identities, *plural*,

with ecclesial identity can neither express nor produce unity unless we consider unity to be a reductionist uniformity or separated but tolerant side-by-side existence.

122. If conversion to unity is essential to ecclesial identity — and it is so, according to the confessions of faith of all the churches — it calls for reversing and transcending historical positions which, on this point at least, are considered to be erroneous and sinful. *Divisive confessional pluralism can only be provisional; it calls for conversion to a confessional pluralism compatible with ecclesial unity.* This development implies the acknowledgment that the church in its separate confessional forms is marked by sin. Ecclesial conversion to unity calls for such an admission on the part of the confessional churches, which makes it possible to emerge from the confessionalist status quo. In fact as soon as Christians recognize that their confessional church lacks ecclesiality because of division, the process of ecclesial and confessional conversion to full catholicity becomes possible once again.

123. For contemporary Protestant ecclesiology, this turn-about means rediscovering that the visible church is not only a sinful historical community, but is also intended by Christ as the *one* and *holy* church. The tradition of the churches of the Protestant Reformation may find among its own Reformers of the sixteenth century the theological elements necessary for the rediscovery of these two "marks" of the church. Unity and holiness are not only the characteristics of the church invisible, but are also to be lived out in the historical and confessional reality of the visible church.

124. For Catholic ecclesiology this turn-about means rediscovering that which was the initial inspiration of the Catholic reformation, beyond its later debasements in the form of "Tridentinism". It consists in recognizing that the church is not just a hierarchical structure and an institution, but is in its essence a *mystery*: the gift of Christ through whom salvation comes to us. It implies that the consistency of modes of behaviour and practices with the gospel message is not just something to be affirmed verbally. It calls us to go beyond too narrow or exclusive a sense of "catholicity" and "apostolicity"

which must above all be measured against this mystery of the church which Christ intended to be *one* and *holy*. All who bear the name of Christians are called to live in unity and holiness.

III. THE ECUMENICAL MOVEMENT: CONVERSION UNDERWAY

a) Conversion at the source of the ecumenical movement

125. The ecumenical movement born in the nineteenth century does not represent a completely new beginning. It has its roots, since the schism between the East and West and the split in the Western church in the sixteenth century, in the hearts of Christians of different confessions. These people were filled with the concern for reconciliation and had already become aware of the conversions that would have to be effected in order to rediscover full communion. In this connection we may mention the fraternal dialogues between Anselm of Havelberg and Nicetas of Constantinople on the procession of the Holy Spirit and on the papacy (twelfth century). The second council of Lyons (1274) and the council of Florence (1438-45) were convened out of the desire to reunify and reconcile East and West.[58] Their failure in history cannot make us forget the legitimacy of their purpose or the spirit of conversion which inspired some of their supporters.

126. In the West, even before the break was completed, there were the efforts of the consultations of Hagenau, Worms, Regensburg (1540-41)[59] and Poissy (1561), during which leading Catholics and Protestants were in dialogue with each other. Even at the Council of Trent, in its second period (1551-52) there were negotiations to enable Protestant envoys to come and take part in the work of the Council. Reasons of theology, religious politics and simply politics as such prevented the realization of this project. At the time the dynamic of separation on both sides was stronger than that of reconciliation — all the more reason not to forget the efforts which bore witness to an attitude of conversion at that time.

127. The birth of ecumenism, in the modern sense of the quest for full communion among churches, was due to a series

of missionary initiatives, awakenings, and militant student movements eager to "win the world for Christ" which evolved in the Reformation churches. This evangelical and missionary concern drew attention to the scandal of division among Christians and the need for their conversion to unity. The spiritual motivation of the project made itself evident in the establishment of an initial form of a global week of prayer for unity. In this movement the role of pioneers who belonged to a variety of confessions was crucial.[60] The personal conversion of some individuals progressively encouraged that of church groups and, later, confessions. Like conversion to the faith, conversion to full communion has developed through the contagion of witness and example.

128. The end of the nineteenth century saw the creation of the great world confessional alliances.[61] This movement of the Reformation churches towards a wider communion was the fruit of a conversion of the regional or national churches, which thus abandoned an isolation that was contrary to the gospel.

129. Crucial reconciliations between the confessional churches marked the first half of the twentieth century. After the Edinburgh missionary conference (1910) and the first world war, the Malines conversations (1921-26) and the conferences in Stockholm (1925) and Lausanne (1927), among others, called the churches to repentance and conversion. Christian youth organizations provided new leaders for the movement. Among the latter Dietrich Bonhoeffer (1906-45) condemned theologically superficial ecumenism and called for a more profound approach and for the spirit of conversion.[62]

130. The second world war created an even greater awareness of ecumenical urgency for all the churches. In 1948 the process came to a climax with the establishment of the World Council of Churches, which took on the task, according to the terms of its "basis", of working in the service of that "fellowship of churches which confess the Lord Jesus Christ as God and Saviour according to the scriptures, and therefore seek to fulfil together their common calling to the glory of the one God, Father, Son and Holy Spirit". The ultimate aim of the

World Council of Churches is certainly the conversion of all the member churches, even if some of its constitutional provisions may well appear to favour the status quo.

131. In the nineteenth century the Roman Catholic Church remained officially outside this great movement, despite more frequent meetings between Catholics and Protestants in the field. Some interventions by Pope Leo XIII, however, inspired by the theology of the "return" ("unionism") but imbued with a spirit of genuine charity, did discreetly open up the path.

132. In the first part of the twentieth century the official attitude of the Roman Catholic Church was that of isolation and then a hardening in regard to ecumenism. Nevertheless some of the great pioneers of the movement of Christians towards unity were among the members of that church.[63] Thanks to a number of providential encounters, all of them had had a personal experience of conversion to Christian unity. Their witness and activities had prepared the ground for the conversion of the Catholic church, especially with the development of the Week of Prayer for Christian Unity observed in January each year.

133. It was necessary to wait for the convening of the Second Vatican Council to see the emergence of the official and institutional conversion of the Roman Catholic Church to the dynamic of ecumenism. Here again, at the origin of this conversion, was that of a man, Angelo Roncalli. During his various incumbencies as a nuncio he had met Orthodox Christians and had long engaged in reflection with Dom Lambert Beauduin, exiled at the time from his monastery. Having become pope as John XXIII he included in the agenda of the council a primary concern for the unity of all Christians. Despite the great authority of his office, it remained a question whether the council would enter into this point of view and bring to life the changes proposed to it. Many bishops were uncertain about the stance their colleagues would take. When the first vote was taken on how the council should proceed, there was surprise. "When the bishops saw that they were in agreement," wrote Fr Congar, "the Catholic church converted

to ecumenism in a few minutes or at most a few hours."[64] In fact the adoption, almost unanimously, of the Decree on Ecumenism only took place three years later. This thunderbolt of grace, this *kairos*, had brought with it a dynamic impetus for confessional conversion, liberating the Catholic church from all its previous fears. It was a conversion that had been prepared by decades of unpretentious work and fervent prayer.

134. Conversion is not simply at the source of the ecumenical movement. It represents its constantly underlying motivation. When conversion flags, the ecumenical movement stagnates or even goes into reverse. All the Christian confessions and all the Christians in each of them have to keep moving forward in the attitude of conversion. The forms of resistance to the ecumenical movement and to the confessional conversion it calls for are many: a preference for the more comfortable status quo, a fear of losing one's confessional identity and, above all, indifference on the part of the majority. Non-doctrinal factors are still important: the old clichés and fears continually reappear while the gap separating theologians undertaking research, church officials and the majority of the Christian people becomes more pronounced.

These attitudes often express a false idea both of unity and of truth, of identity and conversion.

b) Conversion underway

135. Ecumenical conversion is underway in the church, by three converging routes: symbolic gestures, documents on doctrinal dialogue and finally acts or decisions that commit the churches.

Symbolic gestures

136. The scope of symbolic gestures is wide because of the representative value of those who make them, and because they express visibly and emotively the evolving conversion. Who could remain unmoved by the pilgrimage of Pope Paul VI and the Patriarch Athenagoras to the land of Jesus in January 1964, which culminated in their fraternal embrace of reconciliation? Does that event not take us back to the

brotherly extension of "the right hand of fellowship" between Paul and Peter "as a sign of communion" in that same Jerusalem (Gal. 2:9)? In 1975, Pope Paul VI made the unheard-of and astonishing gesture of kneeling before Metropolitan Meliton, the envoy of Patriarch Dimitrios, to kiss his feet. Considering the Vatican protocol — not so long ago — requiring those favoured with an audience to kiss the feet of the pope (which almost caused the meeting between the Orthodox Patriarch Joseph II and Pope Eugene IV to fall through on the eve of the Council of Florence), how can we fail to rejoice that so ambiguous a gesture of homage to authority should be reversed and suddenly find its evangelical meaning, that of Jesus washing the feet of his disciples and inviting them to wash each other's feet?

137. Among symbolic gestures we may also recall the confession by Paul VI at the beginning of his pontificate, addressed to all the "separated" Christians:

> If we are in any way to blame for that separation, we humbly beg God's forgiveness and ask pardon too of our brethren who feel themselves to have been injured by us. For our part, we willingly forgive the injuries which the Catholic church has suffered, and forget the grief endured during the long series of dissensions and separations. May the heavenly Father design to hear our prayers and grant us true brotherly peace.[65]

138. The major meetings between church leaders are also symbolic gestures of conversion and reconciliation. The decision of Michael Ramsey, Archbishop of Canterbury, to go to the Vatican to meet Paul VI (1966) is one of these. On that occasion the pope presented him with his pastoral ring. Likewise the visit of Pope Paul VI to the World Council of Churches in Geneva (1969), followed by the invitation to John Paul II by the WCC (1984) and the latter's visit to the Lutheran church in Rome (1983) on the occasion of the 500th anniversary of the birth of Luther. And how many more! In a category of its own, which is not part of the ecumenical process in the strict sense, the Assisi encounter (1986), in which the representatives of the great religions of humanity met together to pray

for peace in the world, was also a common gesture of conversion. For Christians also have to experience together a conversion to charity and respect towards their brothers and sisters who are believers of other faiths.

139. Symbolic gestures do not take place only at the top. And even these were made possible thanks only to the numerous gestures of conversion which Christians who are still separated had made at the grassroots. Usually these latter gestures have value only for those who experience them. Thus it is impossible to list them here, whether they were made by individuals, local congregations or regional leaders.

140. In May 1989 the European Ecumenical Assembly in Basel on Justice, Peace and the Integrity of Creation represented a symbolic communal event. Convened jointly by the Conference of European Churches (CEC) and the Council of European Catholic Bishops (CCEE), it enabled Christians, both lay and ordained, from practically all the churches of Western and Eastern Europe to live, pray, celebrate and enter into dialogue together for the first time. With the passage of time this event appears, because of its exceptional atmosphere of freedom and loving fellowship, like a prefiguring of the great movement of liberation of the peoples of Eastern Europe which began at the end of 1989.

141. These symbolic gestures which are the product of a conversion become in turn generators of the spirit of conversion. They encourage and embolden Christians of every confession to be involved in a similar process. As such these gestures are indispensable for the dynamics of unity.

Doctrinal dialogues

142. The merit of the Commission on Faith and Order, and then of the WCC, is to have paved the way for a multilateral doctrinal dialogue among the different Christian confessions. A period of slow maturing was needed before it was possible to publish significant documents — especially the convergence document on *Baptism, Eucharist and Ministry* adopted in 1982 at Lima and submitted to all the churches as a call for their conversion.

143. On the Roman Catholic side, the conversion to ecumenism of Vatican II was not implemented only in the drafting of the decree on "the restoration of unity among all Christians" (*Unitatis Redintegratio*). It was a continual concern in the drafting of all the council's documents. While the observers from the other churches did not take part officially in the discussion, they were regularly consulted and were able to give their reactions to the different drafts. The editing commissions always took full account of what they said. From this standpoint, the texts of Vatican II are already the products of an initial doctrinal dialogue. The conversion which led to a full recognition that the "separated brethren" were Christians opened the way to another conversion, that of the understanding. It made possible a new era in theological reflection, in which the spirit of controversy yielded place to kindly consideration of the doctrinal position of the partner. Whereas once each tried to show the others that they were wrong, from then on they have tried to go along with the share of truth of which his brother or sister is the bearer.

144. The documents of Vatican II represented only a beginning for the Roman Catholic Church. After the council it set up a large number of bilateral commissions with different Christian alliances or confessions. This long-term dialogue is still going on. The Catholic church also takes part in the multilateral work of Faith and Order. Some confessions have also organized bilateral dialogues (Lutheran-Reformed, Anglican-Orthodox, Lutheran-Orthodox, etc.). These encounters, patiently repeated, have woven new links of esteem and friendship among the participants, and generally take place in an atmosphere of common concern and prayer. The spiritual conversion of each person grows in them and finds its fruitfulness in the doctrinal conversion which makes it possible to sweep away certain points of contention that have no real basis and to see the real points of dispute in a new light. Considerable doctrinal convergence has already been achieved in the areas of salvation and justification by faith, the church and ministries, baptism and eucharist. In the vast common enterprise of doctrinal ecumenical dialogue the Groupe des Dombes

Acts and decisions that have been taken

145. Among the decisions taken, the first to be mentioned must be the lifting of the excommunications between Rome and Constantinople effected in 1965 by Paul VI and Athenagoras. The Leuenberg agreement (1973) between Lutheran and Reformed churches of Europe also includes a removal of anathemas, as does the document resulting from the Lutheran-Mennonite dialogue of 1980 in France.

The work of the joint German commission on the mutual condemnations by Catholic and Reformation churches in the sixteenth century leads one to observe that most of these condemnations no longer apply to the partners in their present situation. The reasons of yesterday can no longer justify such anathemas today.[66] Mutual lifting of the condemnations of the past would be a far-reaching gesture of ecclesial conversion in which the partners' confessional identities would no longer be defined as in opposition to each other.

146. The recognition of the ecclesial nature of another confession is also a decision for conversion. Thus the Catholic church no longer talks of "heretics" and "schismatics" but of "separated brethren". It no longer considers that in the communities that have separated from it there are only "vestiges of the church": it talks of "churches" or "ecclesial communities" (Vatican II). The Extraordinary Roman Synod of 1985 spoke of an "ecumenical communion of churches". Pope John Paul II spoke of "Christian churches" when he travelled to the Lutheran countries of Scandinavia (1989).

147. Among the acts in the process of ecumenical conversion it is important to stress the role of the reception of the documents of ecumenical agreement or convergence. Here the term is not taken in its canonical but in its theological sense: it is a question of the welcome given in practice to these documents in the thought and life of the members of each church. The preface to *Baptism, Eucharist and Ministry* put it this way: "As concrete evidence of their ecumenical commitment, the

churches are being asked to enable the widest possible involvement of the whole people of God at all levels of church life in the spiritual process of receiving this text."

148. It is not simply a question of receiving a written document. Long ago St Francis of Sales used to recall the difference between musical notation and music that is sung. The text that is received must be able to represent a genuine "score", making it possible to sing the libretto or play the piece on every level of the church's life. Only the responsible authorities can take official ("canonical") decisions to receive a document. But they can do nothing so long as a de facto reception has not taken place among the whole membership of the churches. The process of reception is in this case a conversion process.

149. The increase in the number of councils of Christian churches in the world, including in those countries with a Catholic majority such as France (in 1987), is also an act of conversion and the crossing of a threshold towards mutual recognition.

150. Parallel to the stances and actions which have just been recalled, the development of research in the biblical sciences[67] and the collaboration of Christians of different confessions in the movements of social Christianity[68] have stimulated ecumenical dialogue and the spirit of conversion. Thus we arrive at a fair number of expressions of unity: the celebration of the Week of Prayer in January, social welfare initiatives, joint chaplaincies (in hospitals, prisons, the military and among confessionally mixed families, etc.), ecumenical translations of the Bible, pulpit exchanges, the invitation of observers to the deliberative bodies of each church, etc.

c) Balance-sheet

151. Throughout our century the ecumenical movement has been and remains characterized by the problem of the compatibility of identity with conversion.

152. This long progression of confessional conversions aimed at leading the church towards unity is far from complete. It has to focus on many points of doctrinal controversy which

remain unresolved. Today the question of "models of unity" is already being raised. A variety of scenarios have been proposed under various labels: "organic unity", "conciliar fellowship", "ecclesial communion", "reconciled diversity", and so on, which moreover have some similarities to each other. At the heart of this reflection we find once again the whole dialectic of identity and conversion.

153. For our part, on the basis of the analyses we have just carried out, we see the ecumenical movement as a great process of conversion and reconciliation of our diversities in the quest for communion among confessional identities which, once cleansed of their unevangelical or sinful elements, can receive each other, become complementary and enrich each other. Difference is legitimate within *koinonia* (communion). Thus the churches are invited to arrive at a common recognition of what distinguishes legitimate differences from separative divergences.[69] Confessional identities are not to be abandoned, but to be transformed. Such a vision aims at always linking the concern of unity with that of mission. It is received as faithfulness to the Spirit who leads us forwards.

154. This set of soundings, made in an ecumenical spirit, has taken only some aspects of church history into account. But the intention was to respond to the appeal made on the one hand by Lukas Vischer and on the other by Pope John Paul II, that the history of disunity be studied in a spirit of confessional conversion and contribute to the cleansing of our memories:

> We need a new awareness of the past. Despite the ecumenical movement we still tell the history of the church in terms of the criteria that come from our own traditions. Is it possible to understand and write the history of the church in a way which enables all the churches to recognize themselves in it?... We can only live in one and the same tradition if we succeed in verifying its existence through the centuries in a common presentation of the history of the church. The history of the other churches must begin to form part of our own history.[70]

> The fact that we have different ways of judging the complex events of past history and the differences that continue to exist in some central questions of our faith must not divide us perma-

nently. Above all, the memory of past events must not limit the freedom of our present efforts aimed at repairing the damage caused by these events. The purging of memory is a prime element in ecumenical progress. It involves frank recognition of the wrongs done to each other, and of the mistakes made in the way we have reacted towards each other, while we all intended to make the church more faithful to the will of its Lord. Perhaps the day will come, and I hope it will be soon, when the Catholics and Protestants of Switzerland will be in a position to write the history of this troubled and complex era with the objectivity that is conferred by profound fraternal love. Such an achievement will make it possible to entrust the past unreservedly to the mercy of God and, "straining towards what lies ahead" (cf. Phil. 3:13) to be in all freedom to make it more in conformity with his will, which is that his people will have but one heart and one soul (cf. Acts 4:24,32) to unite in the proclamation and "praise of his glorious grace" (cf. Eph. 1:6). In fact, for each Christian there must be that deep and continuous conversion of the heart, and for each community there must be a constant effort to renew itself in a more profound faithfulness. I am convinced that the foundations necessary for personal and communal ecumenical commitment lie there.[71]

Part III
The Witness of Scripture

155. Inasmuch as the whole of scripture witnesses to the centrality of conversion, it was neither possible nor desirable to undertake an overall review of the scriptural evidence. We thought it more fruitful to verify by a number of soundings whether there is a good foundation for our basic intuition that the call for a conversion inherent in identity has its roots and justification in scripture.

Without misjudging the historical distance and the difference in situations, which forbid us any specious harmonizing, the similarities that can be pinpointed are appeals that have binding force for us, rather than just being encouraging signs.

a) Repentance and conversion

156. In this work the Groupe des Dombes uses the terms "conversion" and "*metanoia*" as equivalents.[72] This usage brings into the term "conversion" the elements of meaning that derive from two families of Greek words: *epistrephein* and *metanoein*.

Metanoein and its derivatives and the Hebrew root they usually translate in the Greek Old Testament mean "renounce" or "repent". The New Testament limited the scope of the meaning of *metanoia* to the act of renouncing a way of thinking or acting regarded as bad. In the New Testament it is people who can repent, while in the Old Testament God himself also repents (Gen. 6:6f.; Jer. 18:8-10; Jonah 3:9).

In the New Testament *epistrephein* and its derivatives and the Hebrew root they generally translate in the Greek Old Testament mean "come back", "return", "turn to", "be converted", and are used in both the secular and the religious fields.

157. Repentance does not come of itself. It is the response to a call (Matt. 3:2; Mark 1:15; Acts 2:38). In Matthew and Mark that call is the first word uttered by Jesus (Matt. 4:17; Mark 1:15). Repentance is the act of human beings who respond to that call, but it is also a gift of God (Jer. 31:18; Acts 5:31; 11:18). In the book of Jeremiah the two actions are linked: human repentance can take place only thanks to God's action.

158. Repentance and conversion are linked twice in the New Testament: "Repent therefore and turn to God so that your sins may be wiped out" (Acts 3:19); and the nations have to "repent and turn to God and do deeds consistent with repentance" (Acts 26:20). It is a way of saying the same thing twice but with a nuance: conversion depends on repentance. Repentance indicates the decision, conversion its implementation.

The two terms are applied to the Jews (Acts 3:19 and 26:20) and to the Gentiles (Acts 26:20). They are used for initial conversion to God and for the ongoing conversions of believers.

The subject of conversion may be individual (Jer. 15:19; Luke 22:32) or collective (Jer. 3:10; Acts 9:35). The same is true of repentance; it is individual (Jer. 8:6; Luke 15:7) or collective (Jer. 31:19; Acts 2:16).

b) Identity and identities

159. While the vocabulary of repentance and conversion occurs in scripture, the word "identity" does not appear there. But its reality is present.

On the one hand, identity is essentially a name given when one is addressed: it is a calling, and often a promise. It becomes effectual when what lies in the name is brought into play. This is true both for individuals and for groups: John means "the Lord is gracious"; Jesus means "the Lord saves"; Israel means "the one who fought with God", which is said of Jacob and of the people (Gen. 32:28); church means "that which is addressed and called"; Christians are those who appeal to the authority of Christ (Acts 11:26).

160. Name and identity are linked to the point that a change of name means a change of identity. Abram becomes Abraham; "Not my people" becomes "My people" (Hos. 1-2; cf. 1 Pet. 2:10; Rom. 9:25); Simon becomes Peter. Likewise the Christian is given a new identity as one who bears the name of Christ. This existence can be defined only in terms of one's total dependence on Christ (cf. Gal. 2:19f.).

161. Moreover, identity is also defined by recognition of the call of God. Individuals or groups acknowledge their identity by confessing God. Confession is correlative to calling (Ps. 95:7; 100:3; Rom. 10:9-13).

Confession of faith is at the same time an invitation for everyone to acknowledge God and live out the identity of believers. This invitation goes out to the ends of the earth (Ps. 96:1-3; 148; Acts 1:8).

162. Within the church there are groups with different identities, such as Jewish Christians and Gentile Christians. In Ephesians 2-3, the author, a Christian of Jewish origin, addresses Christians of Gentile origin as the "nations". Even as Christians the latter keep their cultural identity and do not have to be circumcised and live as Jews. Those people who belong to the "nations", once they have become believers, are fellow-heirs and form one body with the Jewish Christians: "the Gentiles have become fellow heirs, members of the same body, and sharers in the promise in Christ Jesus through the gospel" (Eph. 3:6). Ecclesial unity respects the identity of the existing groups. Through reconciliation with God the difference is no longer divisive, and reconciliation is also achieved between believers of different origins:

> For he [Jesus] is our peace; in his flesh he has made both groups into one and has broken down the dividing wall, that is, the hostility between us. He has abolished the law with its commandments and ordinances, that he might create in himself one new humanity in place of the two, thus making peace, and might reconcile both groups to God in one body through the cross, thus putting to death that hostility through it (Eph. 2:14-16).

This mutual recognition is a constitutive element of the church.

163. This way of being in the church is in tension with another which can be identified in Acts 15. According to this passage certain Jewish Christians wanted to compel Gentile Christians to be circumcised and to live in accordance with Jewish regulations. This requirement was a challenge to the identity of the Gentile Christians. What made it possible to resolve the conflict was recognition of what God had done (Acts 15:8-10) and a re-reading of scripture (vv.15-17). Gentile Christians were recognized as believers, respect being paid to their origin. The Jewish Christians abandoned imposing their requirements on them, and they, for their part, gave up practices which were offensive to the identity of the Jewish Christians. The identity of each was converted through these acts of renunciation. Christians of Jewish origin gave up identifying the gospel with their demands, which were only a particular way of living out the gospel. Gentile Christians gave up what could seem to be idolatry (eating "food sacrificed to idols"), discovering that freedom does not happen without limitations. Freedom and obedience then both appeared in their gospel genuineness. The basic identity grounded in the gospel shone through their respective conversions.

c) Identity, renunciation and conversion

The example of Christ

164. Such acts of renunciation are in line with Christ's own experience. In him the loving freedom of God underwent its "conversion"; that is, God's turning towards human beings in accordance with what the hymn in Philippians 2:6-11 proclaims:

> [Jesus Christ] who, though he was in the form of God,
> did not regard equality with God
> as something to be exploited,
> but emptied himself,
> taking the form of a slave,
> being born in human likeness.

> And being found in human form,
> he humbled himself
> and became obedient to the point of death —
> even death on a cross.
> Therefore God also highly exalted him
> and gave him the name
> that is above every name,
> so that at the name of Jesus
> every knee should bend,
> in heaven and on earth and under the earth,
> and every tongue should confess
> that Jesus Christ is Lord,
> to the glory of God the Father.

165. Jesus Christ renounced the prerogatives which were by nature his. He who was in the form of God freely took the form of a slave. A threefold self-abasement reveals this: becoming a man among human beings, making himself their servant to the end, giving himself up wholly to his God and Father, even to the cross. That gesture was a submission to the will of God, a renunciation of every claim to autonomy, trusting the Other and the others, and giving himself to him and them. Thus Jesus made manifest the different nature of the love of God, going so far as to undergo the "humiliation" of the cross so that God's identity might be revealed and exalted.

His attitude is the very opposite of humanity's initial attitude in their sinful desire for a spurious identity — "you will be like God [or gods]" (Gen. 3:5) — based on absorption or exclusion, fusion or schism, delusion and falsehood. Adam was laying claim to an identity without renunciation and without conversion to God.

166. Through this renunciation God granted to Jesus passage from death to life and allowed him to receive his full identity as Lord, signified in "the name that is above every name", confessed by the whole universe "to the glory of God the Father". God turned him who had turned towards humanity in self-denial back towards himself in glory. Thus Jesus completed the full cycle of identity through renunciation, a

pilgrimage which it then becomes important for the ecclesial community to make its own (Phil. 2:1-5). For this gift and this turning — "conversion" — by God to human beings, achieved in the kenosis of the man Jesus, make possible and already bring about the conversion of human beings from pride and their renunciation of every claim to make themselves, by themselves, the image of God.

167. This turning of God towards human beings shows up in those manifold gestures of turning by Jesus towards those whom he encountered, in which a bodily movement expresses the gesture of acceptance or calling, of love or forgiveness. Jesus turns towards the disciples of John who seek him (John 1:38), towards the woman with the haemorrhage (Matt. 9:21f.), towards those who have the blessing of seeing his ministry (Luke 10:23), towards the crowds who follow him (Luke 14:25), towards Peter, who has just denied him, to fix his gaze on him (Luke 22:61), towards the "daughters of Jerusalem" on the road to Calvary (23:28). This movement of turning calls for reciprocity. Mary Magdalene, for her part, turns twice towards her master to recognize him (John 20:14-16).

168. This process of renunciation is set in a faithfulness which defines the contours of it. Far from giving up his filial relation to the Father, which made him what he is, Jesus displayed it in its primordial truth and made it a reality as a man by his earthly pilgrimage.

Likewise Christians may renounce some elements of their identity which they consider important, but not those which are at the heart of their confession of faith. There are some instances where renunciation would be suicidal. "By this you know the Spirit of God," says the first epistle of John. "Every spirit that confesses that Jesus Christ has come in the flesh is from God, and every spirit that does not confess Jesus is not from God. And this is the spirit of anti-christ" (4:2-3). One cannot renounce the Spirit through whom Christ is confessed in fullness. The confession of faith not only brings together the elements in Christian identity but also defines its boundaries (cf. also Gal. 1:8f.; 1 Cor. 12:3).

The biblical images of conversion

169. If renunciation is not the loss of identity, neither is the process of repentance and conversion. On the contrary, it is the renewal and indeed the transfiguration of identity. This may be illustrated from the many passages in the Bible which are in effect parables of conversion.

170. Joshua 24 tells us of an event of conversion, even if the specific vocabulary of conversion is not used. Israel is called upon to renounce idols and choose the Lord: "Now therefore revere the Lord and serve him in sincerity and in faithfulness; put away the gods that your ancestors served beyond the River and in Egypt, and serve the Lord" (v.14). In making that choice Israel reveals itself as the people of God, led by him from the start (vv.2-13 and 16-18). It can lay hold of its past and open itself to the future. Its full identity is thus accessible to it.

171. In 2 Kings conversion is presented as a return of the people and its religious institutions to God in accordance with the Law: "Before him [Josiah] there was no king like him, who turned to the Lord with all his heart, with all his soul, and with all his might, according to all the law of Moses" (23:25). By renouncing the idolatry revealed by the Law the people rediscover that which constitutes their identity, that is, their bond with God who gave them birth and to whom they belong. Observance of the Law is the reference by which they can identify their divergences and their fidelities, and reappropriate their identity as the people of the covenant (cf. also vv.1-3). This passage also shows the role that can be played by a few officials — the high priest Hilkiah, the secretary Shaphan, Huldah the prophetess and King Josiah — in the conversion of an entire people and its institutions (see the whole of 2 Kings 22-23).

172. Among the parables of forgiveness in Luke's gospel (Luke 15) that of the Prodigal Son can be read as a story of a lost and rediscovered identity. The younger son claims the rights of his identity as a son by asking for his inheritance. In the process he loses it: in the "distant country" he is no longer anyone's son and he becomes the starving slave of a foreigner. When hunger makes him "come to himself", he realizes that he

has lost everything, and his desire is to find at least the identity of a well-treated worker. Thus his repentance takes shape in the turn-about which makes him go back along the entire road which had separated him from his father. The moment of his confession is the moment when his father begets him afresh, treating him as his son who has come back to life, and giving a feast in his honour. The lost identity has been found again.

The older son who stayed at home has to all appearances retained his identity as a son. But for him it has become a right to be claimed. By refusing to recognize his brother in the man whom his father has welcomed back as his son, he in turn loses his own identity as a son. But once again the father goes out from the house: just as he had gone to meet his younger son he comes out to beg the elder to convert to a genuine filial attitude by recognizing in turn as his brother the one whom he calls "your son".

173. In Revelation, a church is called to repentance through the angel who represents it: "Repent then. If not, I will come to you soon and make war against them with the sword of my mouth. Let anyone who has an ear listen to what the Spirit is saying to the churches. To everyone who conquers I will give some of the hidden manna, and I will give a white stone, and on the white stone is written a new name that no one knows except the one who receives it" (Rev. 2:16f.). Confession of faith does not exempt the church from continually repenting by returning to its attachment to Christ. Repentance leads the church also to its final confessing identity, given symbolically to "everyone who conquers" in the stone on which is written the name that is confessed (v.17).

The strength and weakness of identities

174. According to Matthew 16:18 Jesus said to Peter: "You are Peter, and on this rock I will build my church." He had given Simon the name of his new identity; he had indicated his unique role in the founding of the church. Such was his grace, such was his "strong point". But immediately afterwards Jesus treats him as Satan, the tempter, because Peter opposes the announcement of the passion. Whatever meaning our churches

may give to the authority conferred on Peter, we observe that this same Peter, appointed as the foundation of the church, behaves like a tempter towards his Lord. Thus Peter's new identity, which is his strength, leaves him vulnerable to weakness. This is why Jesus speaks to him again, indicating that his thoughts are not the thoughts of God, and calls on him to come after him and follow him.

We may say that what is called for from Peter is a conversion. In so far as we recognize that this passage relates not only to Peter but also to the life of the church, can we dismiss the warning which is part of it?

175. Likewise in Matthew 18:20, Jesus says that "where two or three are gathered in my name, I am there among them". This saying is given special status in some churches to the point of being sufficient authority in their eyes for their ecclesial identity.

But this is to forget that fraternal communion is not established without conflict, reconciliation and regulation. It isolates the saying from the verses preceding it, which invite us to listen to the church and which define its authority: "If another member of the church sins against you, go and point out the fault when the two of you are alone. If the member listens to you, you have regained that one. But if you are not listened to, take one or two others along with you, so that every word may be confirmed by the evidence of two or three witnesses. If the member refuses to listen to them, tell it to the church; and if the offender refuses to listen even to the church, let such a one be to you as a Gentile and a tax collector. Truly I tell you, whatever you bind on earth will be bound in heaven, and whatever you loose on earth will be loosed in heaven" (Matt. 18:15-18). If we find a basis for ecclesial identity in the saying in Matthew 18:20, can we forget the institutional context in which it is included?

176. Likewise Paul was the object of an exceptional calling. The Risen Christ had appeared to him; he had had the privilege of visions and revelations; he had been "caught up to the third heaven". His being called was the basis of his identity as an apostle. But he knew the risk of pride which is attached to all

these gifts. Thus he rejoiced in experiencing weakness and the thorn in his flesh (2 Cor. 12:7). Hence he did not dare boast except in his weaknesses. That experience had already enabled him to warn the Corinthians that "if you think you are standing, watch out that you do not fall" (1 Cor. 10:12).

177. *Thus the strongest point in our identity is also that which is most vulnerable to temptation. We can live truly in accordance with our identity only in a continuous process of conversion.* In pursuing our research, these passages from scripture have been an illumination for us.

d) Balance-sheet

178. This brief biblical survey has progressively inter-related identity and conversion and verified in its own way that conversion is the very opposite of a loss of identity. As people of God, body of Christ and temple of the Spirit, the church is invited to repentance as that which will lead it to its final identity. Knowing how difficult it is for Christians to understand that conversion is not only something done by each member of the church but by communities as such, we are thus helped by scripture to grasp the depth of this conversion to which we are called in Jesus' words to Peter: "When you grow old, you will stretch out your hands, and someone else will... take you where you do not wish to go" (John 21:18).

Part IV
Final Recommendations

179. In this final part of our work we shall try to define, from three different but converging points of view, the positive developments which progress in confessional conversion demands of our churches. We shall begin with a spiritual setting by reflecting on the four marks of the church: we shall then ask for a conscientious examination of our respective temptations; finally we shall propose a few more specific and practical points.

I. THE FOUR MARKS OF THE CHURCH: INVITATION TO CONVERSION

180. We should like to suggest a re-reading of the four marks of the church which are intrinsic to the faith of Nicea, as expressed in the Nicene-Constantinopolitan creed: *one, holy, catholic, apostolic*.

181. An initial comment is essential: Only "one" and "holy" are scriptural expressions. "Catholic" and "apostolic" are derivative marks, whereas *unam sanctam* is a kind of definition of the church in line with scripture.

182. There is a profusion of biblical passages: unity founded on Christ, the one foundation (1 Cor. 3:10-13); the unity of the Spirit in a diversity of gifts (1 Cor. 12); one body in Christ (Rom. 12:3-8); one shepherd and one flock (John 10:16); one as the Father and the Son are one (John 17:20-26); thanks to the unity of the Spirit one in the bond of peace, just as there is "one Lord, one faith, one baptism, one God and Father of all" (Eph. 4:1-6).

183. A passage from Ephesians is also crucial for defining the holiness of the church: "Christ loved the church and gave himself up for her, in order to make her holy by cleansing her with the washing of water by the word, so as to present the church to himself in splendour, without a spot or wrinkle or anything of the kind — yes, so that she may be holy and without blemish" (Eph. 5:25-27).

184. Now — this is a second comment — patristic reflections on the holiness of the church revolve around this passage from Ephesians. They express a marvelling certainty: the holiness of him who alone is holy is communicated through the Son and in the Spirit. That is why the community of sinners is the body of Christ and frail flesh is the temple of the Spirit. That is why there is the communication of holy things — or, better, of the holy mysteries. That is why describing the church as *unam sanctam* means defining it as the communion of saints.[73]

185. We know that no Christian confession professing the Nicene faith can consider this combined mark of unity and holiness as devoid of all meaning. Undoubtedly there are diverging interpretations of it — according to Christian confessions, in the course of history, also within each confession.[74] But when we take another look at history we discover that the debate on the holiness of the church has been the bearer of hope — and hope of conversion — far less than the debate on its unity.

186. On the eve of Vatican II the Catholic interpretation of the unity of the church which could be regarded as classical was that of Moehler: spiritual, mystical and doctrinal unity is expressed in organic unity.[75] This may be interpreted thus: the church in its spiritual unity is Christ in his mystical body, which is also a body of doctrine. Organic unity is Christ in his ministerial and sacramental priesthood, which is fulfilled in the episcopate and through the primacy of the pope.

187. This pattern was not challenged by Vatican II. But it was transformed by the theme of the people of God. The strength of this people does not lie in its gatheredness but in its being called or, rather, in the one who calls them. The church is

that people whom God calls through the grace of his Son and whom he gathers in the freedom of the Spirit. Thus the Spirit has priority over the church, which obliges the church to acknowledge the Spirit's initiative and thus not to set its own bounds.[76] Consequently the ancient formula *extra ecclesiam nulla salus* — no salvation outside the church[77] — acquires a meaning which is no longer the marking out of a limit but the recognition of a wholly spiritual criterion: there is no salvation save in communion and there is no other boundary than the communion of saints. One might equally hazard this description of the church: it is a general summons to humanity for communion with Christ.

188. If the Roman Catholic Church maintains that it is the body of Christ, and if it is convinced that the One Church is inalienably present within it,[78] that claim must bring about a deep and unceasing conversion. In fact, neither incorporation in the church (the fact that one professes the faith, participates in the sacraments and obeys its ministers) nor the membership in the church of all who bear the fine name of Christians has any meaning if the motivation and dynamic do not come from the church's evangelical and missionary orientation. Without that orientation the unity of the church would be a delusion.

189. Secondly, the statement that the church is completely holy in its head, Christ, and that no unworthiness in its ministers is an obstacle to the transmission of that holiness, must not be used to conceal the faults which we should undoubtedly have the courage to call sins of the church. Likewise — and there we come to the third mark of the church — catholicity is sometimes understood too much as a universal expansion of the church of Rome whereas it is in fact that church which has a duty to be catholic by being faithful to its charism. The churches dispersed everywhere are Roman only through the bond of communion with the first of the apostolic churches, that of Peter and Paul. Finally, apostolicity, which is organic continuity with the apostles, takes on its full meaning only through life lived in accordance with the gospel and the preaching of the word.

190. On the Protestant side, while the Reformers and some of their successors maintained the ecumenical creeds and thus the marks of the church, one often sees in practice that *unity* is regarded as an aggregate of diversities which at best tolerate each other, each jealous of its autonomy and its customs; that the *holiness* of the church no longer depends on the holiness of Christ, its head, but on the members' purity of doctrine or life; that *catholicity* has been divested of its dimension of fullness and become nothing more than universality in space, the very use of the term "catholic" being generally rejected; that *apostolicity* consists in a claim to affirm, think and act as the apostles would have done, with hardly any remaining link to the Tradition that guarantees their succession.

191. For this reason we may hope for the following type of theological and spiritual conversion in the interpretation of the four marks of the church:

The Christian confessions must give up the idea of *unity* as uniformity or as a federation; of *holiness* as a canonization of devotion to the ecclesial *res publica* or contrariwise as praise of virtues which are only private; of *catholicity* as a universalism conquering or holding on to conquered territories; of *apostolicity* as a literal return to origins or repetition of beginnings.

192. These temptations must be resisted so that the churches may open themselves up to:
— unity as a challenge to all uniformity and all disparity, in the name of a Christological and trinitarian confession;
— holiness as the obedience of faith, faithfulness to the gospel and listening to the Spirit;
— catholicity as the possibility offered to all persons, whoever and wherever they are, to venture towards truth in its fullness;
— apostolicity as viewing from afar the shore of the kingdom, which the episcopal overseer[79] is pointing out to us and which the beloved disciple was the first to recognize (John 21:7).

193. Thus the God who is greater than our hearts (1 John 3:20), the Christ of mercy[80] and the Spirit who is well-pleased

where truth is a sweet savour[81] will be confessed as the one thing of which there is need (Luke10:42) by the one church.[82]

II. OUR RESPECTIVE TEMPTATIONS

194. As we come to the end of our investigations and of what we have learned, our impression is that the twofold concern with conversion and identity enables us to avoid two false paths in which a quest for unity may go astray:
— The path of one church being absorbed by another. This was long the only path conceivable on all sides, and for some it remains so; one thinks only about one's own identity and sacrifices that of the other.
— The path of the status quo. This is the recent temptation of churches that are content with the state of separation, or of vague relations which are no longer regarded as divisive: it is thought possible to retain the identities of all peaceably, in an existence where there is no conversion.

195. As the witness of scripture has led us to say, the strongest point in identity is also the one most vulnerable to temptation. The only way to live in truth in line with one's identity is in a constant movement of conversion.

Catholics and Protestants could no doubt agree on the affirmation that the charism which makes one church take seriously the exercise of authority in the name of the Lord may lead to an abuse and perversion of authority, and that the charism in some other churches which esteems life in Christian freedom may give rise to a perversion of liberty.

In fact, "the inalienable share of truth"[83] which is present in each church is always liable to be the point of its own perversion. We are thus invited to ask ourselves about where the identity and at the same time the temptation of each church takes root. Ecumenical dialogue has enabled us to discover these places on the basis of the questions we have asked each other.

196. Thus the question for Catholics relates to the understanding and use of authority in their church, which display an

excessive concern to provide institutional guarantees at the expense of the freedom of the Spirit.

Likewise the question for Protestants relates to the understanding and use of freedom in their churches at the risk of confusing all the confessional options with the revelation of the Spirit.

197. The balance between the personal, collegial and community dimensions in the exercise of the ministry within our churches is also threatened, as our previous writings have shown, particularly regarding *episcope*.[84] Among Catholics the personal dimension is the strong point, but it may overlook the necessary complementarity of the collegial and community dimensions, and thus even be perverted. The Reformation churches face a similar danger, some of them granting high status to the collegial aspect (the presbyterian-synodal system), others to the community aspect (the congregationalist system).

198. Regarding the work of the Spirit, it is conceived by Catholics as an irrevocable gift, at the risk of thinking that it excludes all error, while for the churches of the Protestant Reformation it is understood as a promise, at the risk of thinking that it removes all constraint and all security.

199. In general terms Catholicism is so concerned about fullness that it tends to add and include even impurities and syncretism, while the Protestants are so concerned about obedience to scripture that they tend to cut down and suppress, at the risk of falling into purism and abstractions.

200. Finally — and this is an urgent problem — the development of science and technology raises new ethical questions for Christianity.

The Catholic church answers these by referring to a doctrine of creation and through the voice of the *magisterium*, at the risk of sacralizing a concept of natural law disrespectful of the ultimate rights of the individual conscience.

Protestants appeal essentially to the diversity of scriptural witness and to personal responsibility, at the risk of removing all value from the texts as standards and leaving the individual conscience to its own devices.[85]

201. These are some of the questions where it seems that our strong points show themselves to be also the bearers of perversion. Thus we have to ask each other about what we have just called "the inalienable share of truth" of each of our churches. We cannot ignore each other nor exclude each other: on the contrary we are called to encounter each other and correct each other fraternally so that the gospel may not be proclaimed by conflicting voices.

III. FOR A COMPETITIVE APPROACH IN CONVERSION

202. In the field of ecclesiology and the sacraments the Groupe des Dombes has in its previous documents voiced many calls for conversion, which were addressed to each church by its own members.

We do not wish now to repeat the contents of these appeals, but all of us are concerned to tell our churches that the translation of these appeals into practice is a matter of urgency.

We are so bold as to indicate together as Catholics and Protestants some points at which each of our churches must go through a transition in the process of conversion that must lead us to full communion. Finally we shall express a call for a new stage of conversion which concerns them all alike.

a) A call to the churches of the Protestant Reformation

203. Are the churches of the Protestant Reformation drawing all the consequences of their conviction that they belong to the one church of God instituted by Christ? The key terms — *sola scriptura, sola fide, sola gratia* — can open no door other than that of the *sola ecclesia*, which remains the one and only church in its various traditions.

204. That one church is indubitably a eucharistic church, that is, a church of praise and of thanksgiving. The eucharist is not in itself an article of faith, but in St Irenaeus's words it is faith itself *in compendio* — in a nutshell.[86] Consequently the celebration of the word and the Lord's supper together, the

essential act of Christian worship, must be regular and frequent.

205. To stress this character of unity and universality, is it not essential that the term "catholic" be given fresh treatment in the churches of the Protestant Reformation? Unhappily, each confession has arrogated to itself traditional designations that belong to the whole church as a distinctive label: but it is the whole church that is catholic, just as the church in its entirety is evangelical, orthodox and called upon to reform itself. This primordial designation, which speaks of the fullness of Christianity[87] at the same time as its universality, must be recognized in each individual church[88] and cannot be removed from our common history. These divided churches of today are all of them together heirs of the church of the fathers and of the medieval church with its riches and its woes.

206. The churches of the Protestant Reformation rightly claim that apostolic succession is fidelity to the faith of the apostles. Ought they not to listen to the appeal which the Catholic and Orthodox churches address to them regarding the visible continuity which brings ministers into the continuum of the ministry of the apostles?

207. The churches of the Protestant Reformation rightly stress the reality of the priesthood of all who have been baptized. Should they not also recognize the special gift God has given to his church in the person of the ministers of the word and sacraments, the *episcope* and diaconate, in line with the structure of the church instituted by Christ?[89]

208. The Reformation churches cannot forget that the church has to be constantly reformed. Thus they will honour the name by which they are known only if they seek still today to undergo a confessional conversion which snatches them out of the danger of folding themselves up in their own identity.

b) A call to the Roman Catholic Church

209. Will the Roman Catholic Church allow itself to be questioned by the fundamental conviction of the Protestant Reformers that salvation is first of all a free gift of God offered to everyone and that this grace, received from the Father's

mercy, made effectual through the unique sacrifice of the Son on the cross and lived in faith under the influence of the Holy Spirit, is not in the power of any person or of any human authority?

210. The church, which is at once the body of Christ and a visible institution marked by sin, is faithful to its mission only when it recognizes this order of priority, which subordinates it to the free sovereignty of its Lord through the work of the Holy Spirit.

211. If the Roman Catholic Church sees itself as the sacrament of the mediation of Christ, while priding itself in the mystery of its origin, will it nevertheless accept, as a human and historical reality, that it recognize itself as an imperfect, sinful sacrament which contributes to division? In this historical situation of sin, which places it in a fellowship of repentance with the other churches, should the Roman Catholic Church not advance in its recognition of other ecclesial loci in which the unique mediation of Christ is exercised, in the indisputable but impalpable conjunction of the church as the mystery of the body of Christ and the church as a human community? This progress would lead it to understand and affirm with greater humility what it confesses about itself when it says that the true church of Christ "subsists" in the Roman Catholic Church.

212. If each confessional church, and therefore also the Roman Catholic Church which emerged from the Catholic reformation of the sixteenth century, bears its share of sinful responsibility in the divisions from which the ecclesial body of Christ is suffering, has not the church of Rome also in its historical nature lost ecclesial fullness on account of the schisms of the eleventh and sixteenth centuries?

213. The Roman Catholic Church has the fraternal duty to ask the other churches about their ecclesial authenticity; and this enquiry must relate to the faithfulness of these churches to the gospel of Christ, the confessions of faith of the ancient church and the apostolicity of their ministry. But should it not acknowledge that apostolicity, prior to being the expression of an historical continuity, consists first in faithfulness to Christ, the foundation of every ministry, a faithfulness experienced

according to scripture in the diversity of forms and communities of the apostolic age?

214. By respecting that priority and by calling on the churches which arose out of the Protestant Reformation to re-examine their ecclesiality, the Roman Catholic Church could ask them unambiguously about the faithfulness of their ministry to the apostolic tradition. While noting the break in historical continuity made in the sixteenth century, could it not nevertheless recognize the apostolicity of the ministry in the churches which came into being as a result of the Protestant Reformation as well-founded? The path would then perhaps be opened up for a shared conversion to full ecclesial communion, in mutual recognition of the apostolic basis of the ministries on the one hand, and in the non-divisive diversity of expressions of the faith and church practice on the other.

c) A call to all our churches

215. Progress in confessional conversion of the still-divided churches calls now for decisions that will have both real and symbolic value. We mention only a few particularly significant examples.

216. Has the time not come to propose to all Christians a common version of the traditional creeds in languages in which they are not yet available? Achieving this presupposes the effective desire to solve the few problems on which this common version has so far come to grief.

217. The mutual excommunications between Rome and Constantinople have been lifted. Has the moment not come to act in the same way on a large number of anathemas which the churches pronounced on each other in the sixteenth century? Their removal, celebrated liturgically by the leadership in the churches, would show that these anathemas of the past no longer affect the partners of today. It would make it possible to show that a good many points no longer constitute a problem. Following the examples culled from the ancient church, it would demonstrate that the difference between doctrinal terminologies is compatible with unanimity in the faith.

218. Recent ecumenical research has made it possible to define more appropriately the differences that remain within the ecumenical consensus on our ecclesiologies. Has the moment not come to work together at discerning what is a legitimate difference compatible with unity and what is a divisive divergence that must be overcome? Each church would then take the decisions necessary to overcome these divergences.

219. In the field of the doctrine of the faith, many dialogues, multilateral and bilateral, have been undertaken in the last twenty-five years. Even if they still need to be continued, has not the time come not only to draw up a balance-sheet on them but to bring them to a conclusion, that is, to raise their status, whenever possible, from that of documents of interconfessional commissions to the level of new expressions of the faith, which would be authoritative, even if still limited and incomplete, and to draw from them all the consequences for the life of the churches?

220. The progress which has been made towards unity invites our churches not only to pursue resolutely the doctrinal dialogue in which they are already involved, but also to ask each other about the actual behaviour of Christian congregations. It is imperative to recognize that some gestures of reconciliation, the principle of which has been accepted in theory, have still not been put into practice. Even where some elements of agreement have been achieved, they do not always give rise to the ecclesial and confessional behaviour that would be appropriate to them.

221. Many words have been said and many documents written; but too often actions are slow to follow, and this situation becomes worse as the years go on. May our congregations and communities have the courage to confront their practice with the convictions that have already been approved by the ecumenical movement. May they progress as their conversions progress and at the appropriate time celebrate acts of reconciliation which will be symbols of the thresholds that have been crossed. In this way confessional conversion will serve ecclesial conversion and enable the church to give a credible witness to its conversion to Christ.

Appendix
Some Simple Suggestions for Catechesis Where There Is Conversion

Has the day not come when a Roman hand might slip the following into Protestant catechism books so that it might be received with a catholic heart?

1. Members of the Roman church, that is, Christians who belong to that church which was founded by the chief of the apostles and the apostle to the Gentiles, make the sign of the cross of Christ.

In so doing they are not indicating or asking that everyone should do what they do. They are simply confessing that salvation through the cross is given to us in the name of the Father and of the Son and of the Holy Spirit.

2. Members of the Roman Catholic Church apply to Mary the apostle's words: "What do you have that you have not received?" (1 Cor. 4:7). True, they say this using the words of the angel and of Mary's relative Elizabeth: "Greetings, favoured one! The Lord is with you... Blessed are you among women and blessed is the fruit of your womb" (Luke 1:28,42). They consider that what more is said to or about Mary comes not from the Evil One but from the Tradition of the church, in a sort of reading of the scriptures that begins when one closes one's eyes: "Holy Mary, Mother of God, pray for us..." Those who pray in this way sometimes forget to do so in secret, but the Lord's Prayer is their daily bread which they share with all their brothers and sisters.

3. Members of the Roman church celebrate the Lord's supper just as we do. They do not yet celebrate it with us but we can celebrate it with them. On seeing it done, the desire should grow in us for that blessed day when there will only be one bread for the many that we are, and one cup of blessing

which we shall all bless. We can also consider the respect with which they surround the consecrated bread and wine as a sign of the loving faith of the church of God for its Lord offered in communion.

4. Members of the Roman church are never without an entourage of people whom they consider as their spiritual leaders, giving one of them the name of pope. We must learn, and perhaps remind our brothers and sisters, that these people are all bishops, the first among them being the bishop of Rome. In saying this, members of the Roman church affirm that these people have the mission of keeping the churches in continuity with the apostles and in faithfulness to the scriptures. We must consider them as being for our brothers and sisters what our pastors are for us: representatives of God to his church and not creations of the church.

5. Like us, members of the Roman church must be continually converted. They have a great reverence for those who have received the grace to respond "to the end" to this call to "repent and believe in the good news". They think of them as saints, and in worship they thank God for having made of these sinners creatures saved by Christ, intercessors and examples. We may not share this view, and may even ask our brothers and sisters to be faithful to the *Tu solus sanctus* ("you alone are holy") of their own liturgy. But we must never forget that members of the Roman church invoke on our behalf the saint whose name we bear.

6. Because of all this, we must consider members of the Roman church as our brothers and sisters in Christ. We must also recognize that for them this fraternal relation is a desire to do everything so that their own church may not be an obstacle to the practice of that relationship. On the contrary, members of the Roman church expect from that church that its recourse to Peter and Paul will mean the withering away of its Romanness for the sake of the apostolic vitality of the holy church of God dwelling at Rome.

* * *

Has the day not come when a Protestant hand might slip the following into the catechism books of the Roman Catholic Church so that it may be received with an evangelical heart?

1. Protestant Christians, members of a church derived from the Reformation of the sixteenth century, do not think that the church began at that moment, but receive the faith of the fathers and councils gratefully, in solidarity with the ancient church and as a beneficiary of it.

2. Protestant Christians, with the assurance that the word of God preserves the church which keeps that word, nevertheless thinks that the living and genuine tradition of this church must be subordinated to the sole standard of scripture.

3. Protestant Christians, when they confess their faith, not only with the traditional creeds but also with the confessional texts of the sixteenth century — such as the Augsburg Confession, the Confession of La Rochelle or others — consider that it is the confession of faith which gives the church its structure.

4. Protestant Christians, finally, when they confess the one universal church, beyond the visible and institutional forms taken by the historical churches, do not resign themselves to these divisions. In their quest for ecclesial unity in Jesus Christ, they recognize that this diversity is nevertheless not an irreversible obstacle to the realization of unity, and that in a non-divisive plurality, following the example of that of the ecclesial communities in the New Testament, the quest and hope for the kingdom and the righteousness of God may be made manifest.

* * *

Fr Jean-Noël Aletti
Rev. François Altermath
Fr Joseph de Baciocchi
Fr René Beaupère
Rev. André Benoit
Rev. Alain Blancy
Rev. Marc Chambron
Fr Bruno Chenu
Fr Marc Clément
Fr Robert Clément
Fr Irénée-Henri Dalmais

Fr Henri Denis
Fr Michel Fédou
Rev. Flemming Fleinert-Jensen
Rev. Michel Freychet
Rev. Daniel Fricker
Fr Paul Gay
Fr Claude Gerest
Fr René Girault
Fr Étienne Goutagny
Fr Pierre Gressot
Rev. Godfried Hamann

Fr Joseph Hoffmann
Fr Maurice Jourjon
Rev. Guy Lasserre
Rev. Michel Leplay
Rev. Louis Lévrier
Fr Robert Liotard
Rev. Alain Martin
Rev. Alain Massini

Rev. Willy-René Nussbaum
Rev. Jacques-Noël Pérès
Fr Bernard Sesboüé
Fr Damien Sicard
Rev. Jean-Marc Viollet
Fr Pierre Vuichard
Rev. Gaston Westphal

Notes

[1] Cf. the series of theses prepared by the Group from 1956 to 1970 in *Pour la communion des Eglises: L'apport du Groupe des Dombes*, Paris, Centurion, 1988.

[2] Cf. the five documents produced from 1971 to 1985: "Towards a Common Eucharistic Faith" (in *Modern Eucharistic Agreement*, London, SPCK, 1973), "Towards a Reconciliation of Ministries" (in *Modern Ecumenical Documents on the Ministry*, London, SPCK, 1975), "The Episcopal Ministry" (in *One in Christ*, 1978, no. 3), "The Holy Spirit, the Church and the Sacraments" (in *One in Christ*, 1980, no. 3), and one on the ministry of communion (koinonia) in the church universal (in *Pour la communion des Eglises*).

[3] Cf. Marcel Gauchet, *Le désenchantement du monde, une histoire politique de la religion*, Paris, Gallimard, 1985.

[4] This Christian identity may be defined in terms of the minimum required to merit the name of Christian. This was how the "basis" of the WCC was worked out, in a formula which was initially Christological, then formally trinitarian in order to define which religious groups might or might not become members of the World Council of *Christian* Churches; cf. §130.

[5] *Unitatis Redintegratio*, 11.

[6] Cf. §204.

[7] On the origin of this expression see §117.

[8] *Lumen Gentium*, 8.

[9] Cf. the report of the third pan-Orthodox preconciliar conference in Chambésy (October-November 1986), "L'Eglise orthodoxe et mouvement œcuménique", *Istina*, vol. XXXII, 1987, pp.397-400.

[10] Recall for example the tendency of Charles Maurras to contrast Christianity and Catholicism, cf. *Le chemin de paradis, contes philosophiques*, Paris, Flammarion 1920, pp.xxvii and xxviii.

[11] *Loc. cit.*, note 1(7), p.271; cf. *Pour la communion des Eglises*, p.81.

[12] *Loc. cit.*, p.70.

[13] Cf. the comments on the difference between "structure" and "organization" in *Pour la communion des Eglises, loc. cit.*, p. 114.

[14] We recognize that the identity and conversion of the Christian churches cannot be isolated from their relation to the mystery of Israel, but this

15. Cf. §38.
16. Cf. §§24 and 196.
17. The Nicene-Constantinopolitan Creed maintains the same discretion as St Basil regarding the divinity of the Holy Spirit: "We believe in the Holy Spirit, the Lord, the Giver of life, who proceeds from the Father, who, with the Father and the Son, is worshipped and glorified, who has spoken through the prophets."
18. Following the same example in regard to those who rejected the terminology of Chalcedon in the other direction, Paul VI and John Paul II signed with the leaders of pre-Chalcedonian churches Christological confessions of faith which do not use the formula of the two natures of Christ. They thus recognize the full orthodoxy of a Christology couched in Monophysite terminology (cf. *Doc. Cath.*, no. 1633, 1973, p.515, and no. 1880, 1984, p.825).
19. *Doc Cath.*, no. 1499, 1967, col. 1382.
20. Quoted in *Istina*, vol. XXXIV, 1990, p.228.
21. Oration 21, 10; S.C. no. 350, *Discours théologiques*, pp. 95-99.
22. Because Augustine, who from birth was marked with the sign of the cross and tasted of the salt of wisdom (cf. *Confessions*, London, Dent, 1946, I, 11, 17), kept the name of Christ his Saviour in his inmost self (cf. *Confessions*, III, 4, 8). But on the eve of his baptism he was unable to have even an inkling of what the mystery of the Logos made flesh contained (cf. VII, 19, 25).
23. *Ibid.*, III, 4, 7, p.36.
24. *Ibid.*, VIII, 12, 30, pp.171f.
25. *Ibid.*, IX, 4, 11, p.183.
26. *Ibid.*, VII, 19, 25, p.142.
27. *Ibid.*, VI, 4, 5, pp.99f.
28. On Psalm 36, sermon 3, 19-20; *P.L.*, 36, cols 394-395.
29. *Confessions*, I, 1, 1, p.1.
30. *Ibid.*, VIII, 6, 14, p.160.
31. Augustine was the only bishop personally invited by the emperor to the Council of Ephesus, but he died in 430 before it began.
32. Cf. Y.-M. Congar, *L'Église de saint Augustin à l'époque moderne*, Paris, Cerf, 1970, pp.87, 96f.
33. *Ibid.*
34. Marc Lienhard, *Martin Luther, un temps, une vie, un message*, Geneva, Labor et Fides, and Paris, Centurion, 1983, pp.383, 388.
35. *Ibid.*, p.394.
36. *Reformation Writings of Martin Luther*, vol. I, London, Lutterworth, 1952. Translation here by J. Greig.
37. Cf. Louis Pastor, *Histoire des papes*, IX, 1913, pp.102f.; *Histoire des conciles oecuméniques*, vol. 10: *Latran V et Trente*, 1, Paris, Orante, 1975,

pp.168f. Pope John Paul II adopted the words of Pope Adrian VI in his speech to the Lutheran bishops of Denmark on 6 June 1989, *Doc. Cath.*, no. 1988, 1989, p.689.

[38] Certain Protestant Reformers such as Bucer and Calvin took into their ecclesiology some surprising themes, including "Mother church" and "*extra ecclesiam nulla salus*"; cf. Calvin, *Institutes of the Christian Religion*, IV, 1, 7.

[39] Note for example how Martin Bucer refers emphatically to Ephesians 5 in order to call the church to a permanent conversion, so that it may become the body of Christ "without spot or wrinkle". Here Bucer goes beyond the initial ecclesiological concern of Luther who, in the situation of anti-Roman polemics of 1520, reduced the church to the gathering of believers *hic et nunc* to listen to the preached word and the celebration of the sacraments as the "visible" word. In his ecclesiology Bucer sought to locate himself in the tradition of the fathers.

[40] Cf. Calvin, *Institutes*, IV, 1, 12.

[41] With the Catholic theologian Johann Gropper, Bucer drew up the famous "Book of Ratisbon" which presented possible points of agreement for a theological consensus to be discussed at the consultation on unity in Regensburg.

[42] Such as the Czech theologian John Amos Comenius (1592-1670) who was still demanding such a council to bring Christians back to unity. Cf. *Ausgewählte Werke*, Hildesheim/New York, vol. III, 1977, p.46.

[43] Contemporary historiographers talk about the "(Protestant) Reformation" and the "Catholic reform" following on it and in reaction to it. The Catholic reform developed polemical elements which historians refer to as the "Counter-Reformation".

[44] It is noteworthy that at Trent the doctrinal decrees on the one hand and the reforming decrees on the other were discussed so much in parallel that when the council ended in 1563 the conciliar decrees had established a new framework for the activities of the Catholic clergy. See N.S. Davidson, *La Contre-Réforme*, Paris, Cerf, 1989, p.41 ff.

[45] This point is underlined by M.D. Chenu and G. Alberigo; cf. the latter's "Du Concile de Trente au tridentinisme", *Irenikon*, vol. 54, no. 2, 1981, pp.192-210.

[46] "Human beings are disposed towards justice itself, when, being urged on and aided by divine grace, and with the faith they hear preached being formed in them, they turn freely towards God...; when, understanding that they are sinners,... they arise to hope, trusting that God will be favourable to them because of Christ; when they begin to love him as the fountainhead of all justice...; when, finally, they propose to receive baptism, to begin a new life and to keep the divine commandments" (sixth session, Decree on Justification, chap. 6).

[47] Bellarmine defined the church as "the assembly of human beings bound together by profession of the same Christian faith and communion in the

the sacraments, under the government of legitimate pastors and chiefly of the one vicar of Christ on earth, the Roman pontiff. In order to be in some measure part of the true church,... no inward virtue is in our view required, but only the outward profession of the faith and the fellowship of the sacraments, which is something accessible to our senses. In fact the church is an assembly as visible and palpable as are the assemblies of the Roman people or the kingdom of France or the Republic of Venice" (quoted by Congar, *op. cit.*, pp.372f.).

[48] We cited earlier (§89) the confession by Pope Adrian VI. In 1546 Cardinal Reginald Pole, the papal legate for the first phase of the Council of Trent, likewise declared: "We are all to a great extent responsible for the misfortune that has struck us — the rise of heresy and the collapse of Christian morality — for we have not been capable of tilling the field that was entrusted to us. If we do not repent, God will not speak his word to us" (quoted by Davidson, *op. cit.*, p.41).

[49] For instance, in regard to eucharistic doctrine the Council of Trent dealt with only three disputed questions: the real presence and transubstantiation, the legitimacy of communion in one kind and the eucharist as a sacrifice. Clearly eucharistic theology of the period said more than that. A similar point may be made regarding the relation of the priest to the eucharist. To answer the challenges of the Protestant Reformers on the ministerial priesthood, the dogmatic texts of Trent consider the priest as above all a "sacrificer". Here Trent must be corrected by Trent itself, for the disciplinary decrees place enormous stress on the responsibility of the priest and the bishop in relation to the word (cf. A. Duval, *Les sacrements au concile de Trente*, Paris, Cerf, 1985).

[50] We deliberately use the word "believe" with all three objects, though the meaning becomes more analogical from one to the next. This is the well-known theme of the "three whitenesses" (the host, the immaculate robe of the Virgin and the pope's soutane), lavishly embroidered by many preachers.

[51] This formula meant that the confession of the prince (or any other civil authority) had the force of an obligation for all the subjects of the same territory, on pain of exile.

[52] The correspondence between Bossuet and Leibnitz at the end of the sixteenth century on the role of the Council of Trent for Christian unity is one example; another is the exchange in France between Catholic and Protestant theologians on the eucharist (such as P. Noüet and Nicole with Pastor Jean Claude). Conversion of one group to the church was then seen by the others as an individual conversion, in particular on the part of princes, whose conversion implied that of their subjects. Cf. H. Jedin ed., *Handbuch zur Kirchengeschichte*, vol. 5, Freiburg in Breisgau, Herder, 1965, pp.555-570.

[53] The well-known motto *in necessariis unitas, in non necessariis libertas, in utrisque caritas* (unity on what is necessary, freedom on what is not

necessary, charity in everything), often wrongly attributed to St Augustine, probably comes from the Augsburg theologian, Rupert Meldenius, in a book written around 1626: *Paraenesis pro pace Ecclesiae ad theologos Augustanae confessionis*; cf. *Realenzyklopädie für protestantische Theologie und Kirche*, XII, Leipzig, J.C. Hinrichs'sche Buchhandlung, 1903, pp.550-552.

[54] Cf. M. Carbonnier-Burkard, "Une liaison gréco-réformée au XVIIe siècle", in *Foi et vie*, 3-4, July 1990, special issue: "Constantinople aux portes de l'Europe", pp.67-77.

[55] "We are all cosmopolitans, citizens of the same world and, I would add, of the same church." "After such great horrors [=those of the thirty years' war] the time has come to contemplate the conversion of the hearts of all people... You Christians, the people beloved of God, your constant arguments on philosophy, theology and politics prove that you are unaware of your salvation. Oh, the opinions dividing us are countless. Hate and the disorder that are the product of these are endless and beyond measure... This is not God's will; the right way is not to combat discord by discord but to consolidate everything that can be united by unity." Comenius, *Ausgewählte Werke*, pp.25-29 and 115 (212).

[56] Cf. ibid., pp.77 (17); 80f. (26); 93 (36).

[57] Contrary to the commonly accepted view, the expression *ecclesia semper reformanda* seems not to go back to the sixteenth-century Protestant Reformers but to the Pietist Jodocus von Lodenstein (1620-77), who used it around 1675; cf. E. Mülhaupt, "Immer währende Reformation?", in *Luther im 20. Jahrhundert, Aufsätze*, Göttingen, Vandenhoeck & Ruprecht, 1982, p.267.

[58] Cf. §78.

[59] Cf. §91.

[60] To mention only a few names from the nineteenth century and beginning of the twentieth: Jean-Frédéric Oberlin, Tommy Fallot, Pusey, Charles Wood, Lord Halifax, John R. Mott, Marc Boegner, W.A. Visser 't Hooft. We may remember also the part played in the ecumenical movement since 1942 by the Taizé community.

[61] Cf. *Le ministère de communion dans l'Eglise universelle*, Paris, Centurion, 1986, §81.

[62] Cf. E. Bethge, *Dietrich Bonhoeffer: Theologian, Christian, Contemporary*, London, Collins, 1970, pp.181ff.

[63] The names of some who are no longer with us are well-known: Abbé Fernand Portal, Cardinal Mercier, Dom Lambert Beauduin, Abbé Metzger, Abbé Paul Couturier, Father Maurice Villain.

[64] Y. Congar, *Essais oecuméniques*, Paris, Centurion, 1984, p.35; cf. H. Roux, *De la désunion vers la communion*, Paris, Centurion, 1978, pp.215-247.

⁶⁵ In his address at the opening of the second session of Vatican II, 29 September 1963, Xavier Rynne, *The Second Session: The Debates and Decrees of Vatican Council II*, London, Faber & Faber, 1963, p.358.

⁶⁶ Cf. the results of the work of the joint Protestant-Catholic commission formed in Germany after John Paul II's 1980 visit there; *The Condemnations of the Reformation Era: Do They Still Divide?*, Minneapolis, Fortress, 1990.

⁶⁷ Such as the creation of dialogue and research forums like the Society for New Testament Studies (SNTS) in 1938.

⁶⁸ We may recall here the Rev. Wilfred Monod and the Lutheran Archbishop Nathan Söderblom, whose social commitment in the name of the gospel was accompanied by an indisputable ecumenical openness.

⁶⁹ Cf. the Joint Catholic-Protestant Committee in France, *Consensus oecuménique et différence fondamentale*, Paris, Centurion, 1987.

⁷⁰ L. Vischer, "Oecuménisme — chemin de l'histoire", in *Unité des chrétiens*, 51, July 1983, p.9.

⁷¹ John Paul II, speech to the Federation of Swiss Protestant Churches, June 1984, *Doc. Cath.*, no. 1878, 1984, p.726.

⁷² In this section we always translate *metanoia* by "repentance" and *epistrephein* by "convert".

⁷³ The most concise statement of this unity-holiness of the church is undoubtedly Cyprian's formula, adopted in *Lumen Gentium*: "a people brought into unity from the unity of the Father, the Son and the Holy Spirit" (Cyprian, *De Oratione Domini*, 23; *Lumen Gentium*, 4).

⁷⁴ Recall some of the reasons for reticence about the holiness of the church: Is the holiness of Christ, the pattern, not incommunicable and moreover just a little discouraging? Does not this affirmation of holiness turn into worship of the saints and does it not set up the church as a judge of holiness? Is the holiness of the church not solely eschatological?

⁷⁵ Cf. Moehler (1796-1838), *Die Einheit in der Kirche*.

⁷⁶ Cf. Acts 10:47: "Can anyone withhold the water for baptizing these people who have received the Holy Spirit just as we have?" If Irenaeus wrote: "Where the church is, there is the Spirit of God", he also added: "And where the Spirit of God is, there is the church and every grace... And the Spirit is the truth" (*Adversus omnes haereses*, III, 24, 1). In other words, the church is that which the Holy Spirit guides into all truth. This priority of the Spirit over the church was reaffirmed by the sixteenth-century Protestant Reformers.

⁷⁷ Origen, "On Joshua", *Homilies*, 3, 5; *S.C.* no. 71, p.143; Cyprian, *Letter*, 73, 21, 2.

⁷⁸ *Lumen Gentium*, 8: "Haec ecclesia... subsistit in Ecclesia catholica..." ("This church... subsists in the Catholic Church ...")

⁷⁹ On the clear understanding that the term "episcopal overseer" here covers several forms — bishops, presidents, synods; cf. our document "The Episcopal Ministry".

[80] Cf. Hosea 6:6; Matthew 12:7; Irenaeus, *Adversus omnes haereses*, IV,17,4.
[81] Cf. Augustine, *Confessions*, IV,12,18.
[82] Cf. the reading of Song of Solomon 6:9 by Cyprian in *Letter*, 69,2,1.
[83] Cf. the Joint Catholic-Protestant Committee in France, *Consensus oecuménique et différence fondamentale*, n.17, p.25.
[84] Cf. "Le ministère de communion dans l'Eglise universelle", no.9, and "The Episcopal Ministry", nos 42-44.
[85] Cf. Joint Catholic-Protestant Committee in France, "Catholiques et protestants face à la morale dans une société laïque", *Doc. Cath.*, no. 1995, 1989, pp.1072f.
[86] Irenaeus, *Adversus omnes haereses*, III,16,7.
[87] "Religion must be sought among those alone whom we call catholic — that is, orthodox — Christians. They preserve the integrity which they follow in uprightness", Augustine, *De vera religione*, 5,9; *P.L.*, 34, 127.
[88] The letter from the church of Smyrna to the church of Philomelium reporting the martyrdom of Polycarp is of course crucial on this matter. Polycarp in particular is described there as bishop of the catholic church of Smyrna (16,2; *S.C.*, no. 10, p.265).
[89] We understand these words in accordance with the statements in our previous documents, *Pour une réconciliation des ministères* and "The Episcopal Ministry".